MIRIAM SUMMER

Dog training
Impulse Control
— & —
Frustration Tolerance

Beginners

124 Easy Step-by-Step Games
for a Happy and Stress-Free
Life with your Dog

Incl.
21 Brain
Games

ISSUE 1, 2023

TABLE OF CONTENTS

INTRODUCTION... 1

CHAPTER 1
Impulse Control And Frustration Tolerance: Definition 3
    1.1 WHAT IS IMPULSE CONTROL?.. 4
    1.2 WHAT IS FRUSTRATION TOLERANCE? 5
    1.3. EXAMPLES 6

CHAPTER 2
Causes Of Insufficient Impulse Control And Frustration Tolerance 8
    2.1 RACE-SPECIFIC FACTORS 9
    2.2 GENETIC FACTORS... 11
    2.3 STRESS-RELEVANT FACTORS 12
    2.4 THE DOG'S PERSONALITY 16
    2.5 BAD PARENTING 16
    2.6 HEALTH PROBLEMS 17
    2.7 TRAUMATIC EVENTS... 18
    2.7.1 DEPRIVATION SYNDROME 19

CHAPTER 3
Punishment Vs Reward: When To Use What? 21
    3.1 PRIMARY AND SECONDARY REINFORCER 22
    3.2 REWARD AND PUNISHMENT - BASICS.............................. 23
    3.3 CLICKER TRAINING AS A SECONDARY REINFORCER 26

CHAPTER 4
Benefits Of Impulse-Controlled Training.. 29

CHAPTER 5
Frequently Made Mistakes, And Asked Questions............................ 32

CHAPTER 6

Impulse Control And Frustration Tolerance Training........................38

    6.1 Basic Exercises for Self-control and Obedience....................39

    6.2 Housetraining exercises 62

    6.3 Feeding Behaviour 67

    6.4 Leash Handling 74

    6.5 Encounter with other dogs 84

    6.6 My dog is afraid of... 89

    6.7 Stopping your Dog from Jumping at Someone 109

    6.8 Understanding dog language: Barking,

    whining, whimpering...114

    6.9 Biting and snapping 119

    6.10 Hunting Instinct..123

    6.11 Practical city training 127

    6.12 Useful exercises for everyday life, personal hygiene and visits

    to the vet 136

CHAPTER 7

Bonus Exercises: Brain Teaser For Dogs...142

CHAPTER 8

Exercising Plan For Your Dog's First Year..155

CLOSING WORDS 163

DISCLAIMER...173

IMPRINT 174

"He lacked the most important virtue of the educator, PATIENCE. I do not mean that patience which borders indifference and leads to loneliness, but the other. True patience is composed of understanding, humour and perseverance".

Erich Kästner

From the book "When I was a little boy"

INTRODUCTION

Every dog owner wants a calm, stress-free and relaxed life together with their dog. However, knowledge about our animals' frustration tolerance and impulse control is necessary to achieve this. The bitter truth is that there are dogs that react immediately to every stimulus and chase after cyclists, joggers or even cars as if stung by a bee. While others find it extremely difficult to find peace and are so restless and hyper, they seem like Duracell bunnies. When you think of impulse control disorder, you probably immediately have the Border Collie in mind, a dog passionate about playing ball and reacting uninhibitedly to every stimulus.

Dogs that show demanding behaviour, going from zero to one hundred and consistently try to control everything, aren't only nerve-wracking for their owner, they also drain their energy in the process. For this reason, dog owners must familiarise themselves with frustration tolerance and impulse control. In psychology, impulse control means controlling one's feelings and emotions, a disorder where people react impulsively and cannot resist. This same psychological thought applies to dogs too.

Consequently, impulse control disorder is associated with low frustration tolerance, meaning a dog cannot stand it, if its wishes aren't immediately satisfied and struggles to endure certain situations. An example could be a dog that immediately barks when he does get his favourite toy. Also, in cases where a dog cannot stay alone and defends food or other resources, low frustration tolerance and a lack of impulse control can be the reason behind it. The following factors are identified as the causes: lack of socialisation, a genetic disposition, breed, character and upbringing.

Furthermore, breeding can also be of great importance; whether the dog is more easy-going or constantly stressed. Another factor that can make life with a dog very stressful is living in an urban area. The mass of stimuli in an urban environment can be difficult for a dog to process. Some people and dogs have a greater struggle than others. There are many ways to support your dog in establishing reasonable impulse control and high frustration tolerance. In addition to the proper training and mental activity, sufficient rest periods are also part of a happy dog's life. We all want only the best for our four-legged companions. This book is dedicated to researching the causes, behaviour and possible solutions for lack of impulse control and low frustration tolerance.

It's supported by findings that explain why rules and structures are so important in everyday life and why you should encourage your dog according to his genetics. Through this knowledge, you'll learn to understand your dog better and how best to strengthen your bond with him.

At the core of this book are one hundred and twenty-four well-thought-out and easy-to-implement exercises for high frustration tolerance and impulse control.

Furthermore, you'll find a bonus chapter with 21 exercises to mentally and physically optimise your dog for a relaxed, stress-free and happy co-existence with you.

– CHAPTER 1 –

Impulse Control and Frustration Tolerance: Definition

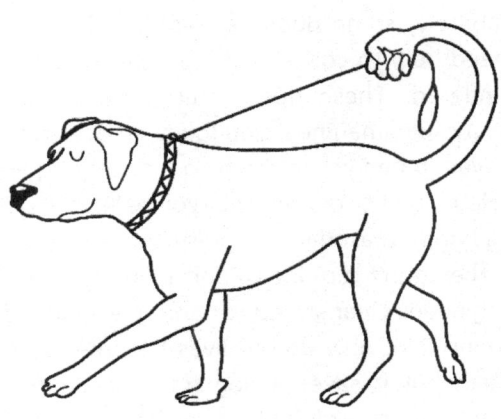

The first chapter of the book is dedicated to the definition and difference between impulse control and frustration tolerance. Knowing both terms is very important to understand better and support your dog more holistically.

1.1 What is Impulse control?

Impulse control is the ability to control one's feelings and consciously react. In concrete terms, this means that a dog - if they've reasonable impulse control - can "control himself". Here I'm referring to the kind of dog that is difficult or impossible to distract. However, if impulse control isn't insufficiently developed, dogs find it difficult to resist temptation.

A dog with little self-control may rush to its food bowl, despite the fact it should patiently wait until its owner gives the OKAY. By following their impulse uncontrollably, they neglect their trained behaviour. Impulse control is essential for a relaxed and stress-free life. Unfortunately, some dogs get distracted by everything and everyone, need help to concentrate and seem to follow their impulses unhindered. These dogs often have fragile nerves and overreact to stimuli. Imagine if you followed every instinct and, for example, stayed in bed in the morning instead of going to work. It might go well the first two times, but you're likely to lose your job if it becomes a habit. Reasonable impulse control is also essential for our dogs so they don't turn into a permanently stressed bundle of nerves. A dog needs clear structures and rules and a defined space to move around. Not only do our lives become more relaxed and uncomplicated, but it saves a dog from becoming a danger to themselves and others. Think of a dog that uncontrollably acts on its hunting instinct - for example, an Australian Shepherd - endangering road users by herding cars, or a Labrador that freely consumes anything edible from the roadside, including poison.

Situations characterised by low impulse control in dogs can pose a significant danger and may lead to undesirable outcomes. Living with a dog that lacks impulse control can also be challenging and restrict your daily life. For example, going for a walk can turn into a nightmare as your dog pulls and tugs on the lead, or taking him to new places becomes difficult because he never seems to settle down. Even visiting a coffee shop can become a nerve-wracking experience. If you find yourself facing such scenarios, your dog likely has a disorder of impulse control combined with low frustration tolerance.

1.2 What is frustration tolerance?

Frustration tolerance describes the ability to endure frustration and not follow one's instinct uncontrollably. Low frustration tolerance is nothing more than the inability to postpone one's wishes and needs them fulfilled immediately. Suppose something doesn't occur; frustration sets in. In psychology, there's this concept of reward deferral, which is linked to frustration tolerance. It means preceding a reward that requires no effort and is immediately available in favour of a better reward.

An example would be a dog about to play with a fellow dog. Its owner calls out; they stop playing the game and go to him because they know they'll be rewarded for good behaviour. So, they choose a reward that requires more effort and fall back on their learned behaviour. This kind of dog has a *high* frustration tolerance.

A typical example of dogs with low impulse control and frustration tolerance is leash aggression, i.e. dogs that constantly pull on the lead. Especially with leash aggression, dogs follow their first impulse: to pull on their lead and bark out of frustration, insecurity or fear. Jumping on people also falls into this category. By lunging at people, these dogs get immediate feedback, namely attention. Whether it's good or bad is irrelevant in this particular situation.

1.3. Examples

Low impulse control is almost always accompanied by low frustration tolerance because one causes the other. There are endless examples of dogs affected by this:

- Not being able to stay alone and suffering from separation anxiety.
- Becoming quickly frustrated when they've to solve intelligence games.
- Gobble down their food, defend resources, and show jealous behaviour.
- Having to be kept on a lead all the time because the hunting instinct is very strong.
- Overly aware of fast-moving objects such as scooters, roller skaters, cars etc.
- They are jittery, nervous, unfocused and can't calm down.
- Turn into ball junkies.
- Yapping, barking and whining to get attention.

Other possible consequences of a lack of impulse control and low frustration tolerance can be hyperactive, fearful, and aggressive behaviour. Be aware that impulse control and frustration tolerance aren't *endlessly available* to a dog. Dogs need a lot of energy to control their impulses. If you have been in town with your dog, he'll have been naturally exposed to a lot of stimuli. Perhaps he's behaved in an exemplary manner and doesn't need a break afterwards. But if you place him in another stressful environment or activity and he reacts impulsively, his impulse control and frustration tolerance has increased. In this case, you cannot blame your dog for his behaviour but recognise that you have overworked him. Dogs always need sufficient rest periods after exciting and over-stimulating activities to process the day's experiences.

The good news is that dogs can always learn impulse control and frustration tolerance. To do this, you need to know the causes of the behaviour. In the next chapter, you'll learn what these are and what breed, genetics, and upbringing have to do with them.

– CHAPTER 2 –

Causes Of Insufficient Impulse Control And Frustration Tolerance

CHAPTER 2

Causes Of Insufficient Impulse Control and Frustration Tolerance

M any causes result in poor impulse control and frustration tolerance, and scientists assume that multifactorial causes play a role in people with common impulse control. It means that not only one factor is responsible for deficits in this area, but also hereditary predispositions, the environment, and stress.

People who suffer from impulse control disorder also show behaviour that can be classified as aggressive and often report inner impulses that they know are of no use to them. But they do it anyway. We must remember that humans usually make this decision to act on an impulse "consciously", whereas dogs work more or less instinctively because they cannot reflect. But what causes dogs to lack impulse control and frustration tolerance? Knowledge of the different causes is the *basis for our training*.

2.1 Race-Specific factors

Breed plays a significant role in impulse control and frustration tolerance. It can often be observed that dogs with a heavier build, such as those categorised as Molossians in cynology, have better impulse control than dogs that fall under the category of herding dogs and driving dogs. It can be attributed to the bulkier build and the fact that these dogs are clumsier and slower. The delicate appearance of a herding dog on the other hand, and the faster metabolism that comes with it can encourage nervous behaviour. However, this is no guarantee that the strong Newfoundland will not have behavioural problems in this area because several factors always work together simultaneously. A lack of impulse control can also occur in heavier dogs due to various causes, such as health problems or trauma.

As already mentioned, dogs classified as **herding dogs** are mainly known for their impulsive behaviour. This breed can vary quickly develop behavioural problems if not appropriately kept. They are incredibly docile and intelligent but can be prone to hyperactive behaviour when kept in the wrong environment. Many think a herding dog, like a Border Collie or an Australian Shepard, needs to be adequately exercised, but that is a misconception. Border Collies tend to develop compulsive behaviour if challenged too much or too little. These dogs first need to learn to rest and not 'huff and puff' every time they move. In a stressful living environment and excessive activity, these dogs can become increasingly hyper, getting on their owners' nerves. and making a stress-free everyday life impossible.

But **hunting dogs** can also lack impulse control because, logically, hunting is in their blood. The owners are often desperate when their dog chases after a rabbit repeatedly and doesn't react to the hundredth recall. For this reason, it's essential to strengthen a dog's impulse control and offer them alternative activities.

Dogs that have both a **protective** and a strong **hunting instinct** are the Pinscher and Schnauzer. Pinschers include the Doberman and the German Pinscher. The Schnauzer section includes all types of Schnauzers and the Russian Black Terrier. These breeds typically have strong self-confidence and a tendency to bark.

The **Molossoid** breeds can also have a strong hunting instinct, such as the Boxer, Dogo Argentino or Hovawart. These breeds belong exclusively in the hands of connoisseurs and experienced dog owners.

The most popular dog breeds are still the terriers, for example, the Jack Russell Terrier, the West Highland White Terrier and the American Staffordshire Terrier. They are considered to be particularly affectionate and playful. One should ensure that these dogs are well-exercised because they need to be occupied with a task. A hunting substitute, general training and lots of impulse control training should be at the top of your to-do list if you want to provide your terrier with a species-appropriate home.

The Golden Retriever and the Labrador Retriever are considered **the prototype** of family dogs. They fall under the category of **retrieving dogs** and they were bred to retrieve a hunter's dead prey. Furthermore, this breed is often trained as assistance and therapy dogs due to their friendliness with humans, willingness to obey, and appealing appearance.

But no matter which breed you choose, dogs must first learn to develop high impulse control and frustration tolerance.

2.2 Genetic factors

Another foundation for lack of impulse control may already have been laid in the bitch's womb. Here, **genetic disposition** plays a decisive role. If the mother has low impulse control and is prone to hyperactive and impulsive behaviour, then there is a high probability that her puppies will also show the same trait. The background is that the bitch's adrenal cortex secretes more cortisol due to her nervous character, and consequently, her puppies are already confronted with the hormone in the uterus. Another favouring factor is the time after birth when the puppies' rearing occur. If the breeder doesn't train the puppies in impulse control and frustration tolerance from the beginning, a vital time stage is lost in which the puppy could learn a lot.

Nevertheless, as an owner, you can influence your dog's personality. Genetics are essential, but a stable environment with praise, positivity and consistent training is even more critical. If an owner radiates sovereignty and fulfils their pet's needs in a species-appropriate way, even a dog that hasn't been genetically favoured can become an all-around happy dog.

2.3 Stress-Relevant factors

Knowing how stress is defined is crucial to understanding the relationship between a lack of impulse control and low frustration tolerance and focus. Each person perceives stress differently and largely depends on personal resilience (psychological resistance). A distinction is made between positive anxiety (eustress) and negative stress (distress). It means that people can perceive a situation differently. Some experience eustress and are motivated; others experience pain and are thus negatively affected. People and dogs who experience negative stress share the same physical reactions: The pupils constrict, the heart rate increases, breathing becomes shallow or accelerates, the human begins to sweat, and the dog pants. Which coping strategies humans or dogs resort to, depends on the character of the upbringing and the environment.

Resilience, as mentioned earlier, also plays a significant role in how people and dogs react to stress. Resilient people automatically have better impulse control because they aren't constantly distracted and have learned how to endure particular situations. Indeed, impulse control correlates negatively with stress. It means that a stressed dog can show little to no impulse control because stress blocks his brain, so he can no longer fall back on learned behaviours. He gets into a kind of tunnel vision and is no longer able to act rationally.

Stress in dogs has many faces. It's essential to recognise and interpret your dog's body language.

Here is a list of the most common symptoms of stress in dogs:

- Crying, wailing, whining, howling
- Jumping up on someone or something
- Shaking
- Pulling or biting on their lead
- Following an imaginary scent trail
- Increased salivation
- Pacing and restlessly walking around
- Chasing their tail
- Nibbling on their paws, chewing on objects
- Licking their snout
- Ejected penis
- Alternately lifting the front paws
- Riding
- Increased pawing
- Eating grass
- Scratching themselves
- Muscle tension
- Mouth odour
- Restlessness, hyperactive behaviour
- Destructiveness
- Dilated pupils, red-rimmed eyes
- Yawning is frequently in succession and often in combination with other stress commands.

This list is only a selection of the possible stress symptoms a dog can exhibit. Like us humans, dogs are different and resort to various stress commands. Moreover, there are conflict strategies that dogs use in certain situations of excessive demands and in response to threats. These are called the **four F's.** Humans also use these strategies to react to conditions or events that make us feel uncomfortable, frightened or stressed. A dog's behavioural reactions are as follows:

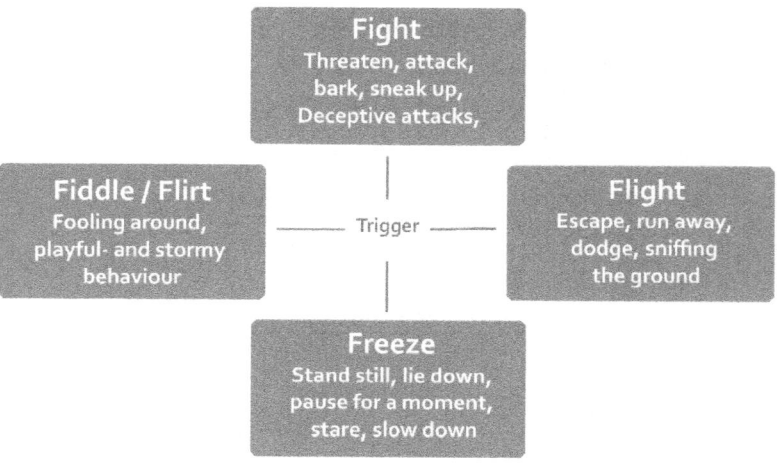

Figure 2: Four F's of stress signs in dogs

- **Fight (threatening and fighting)**

The dog sees no other way out than to move forward and try to drive away the supposed attacker. This strategy is often used in dog encounters. If a dog no longer has the possibility of evading and wants to avoid contact with their fellow dog, it usually resorts to fighting. In urban areas, where many people and dogs live together in confined spaces, it's common to see dogs who have developed lead or leash aggression. When dogs are on a lead, their body language is already restricted from the start. In such a situation, dogs usually give each other space and run an arc. They typically wouldn't approach each other head-on. Unfortunately, this isn't always possible, which is why they go into attack mode or maintain a threatening position. The fight is usually accompanied by barking and growling, and often one dog lunges forward into their lead to make the other dog understand the seriousness of the situation.

- <u>Flight</u>

Under normal circumstances, dogs always choose the de-escalating path, leaving the situation to avoid any conflict. However, due to our urban life, this is very rarely possible. Flight means to escape, but it doesn't (only) suggest that a dog runs away from the situation. But perhaps, he just wants to build up distance. A dog can do this by turning their body away and leaving the situation or location. At times, he may try to crawl away somewhere or even dig his way out of the situation. An example also could be a dog that goes to dog school but doesn't want to or feels uncomfortable in the confined square or circle. He might try digging a hole at the edge of the fence to escape from the situation.

- <u>Freeze</u>

Freezing is also an expected behaviour that dogs may exhibit during unwanted dog encounters. Even from a distance, when a dog notices a fellow dog, he slows down his walking, remains frozen, sits or lies down, and cannot be encouraged to move on. But dogs also show this strategy in other situations, for example, when they see something in the distance that they cannot decipher.

- <u>Fiddle/Flirt (fooling around)</u>

Fiddling is often not perceived as a reaction to a stressful situation.

To humans, a dog may appear to exhibit happy, silly behaviour as if he wants to play. But it's important to recognise that this may be a reaction to a conflict that he wants to resolve without escalating the situation.

In this case, if other stress commands are added, such as yawning, licking their muzzle, etc, humans should intervene and resolve the situation. It's not uncommon for humans to misinterpret fiddling as a game. For example, when two dogs chase another dog through an area and no longer playfully take turns running. This is bullying and is no longer a game but a very stressful situation for the chased dog.

Coping strategies in stressful situations aren't fixed; they can change depending on the situation or flow smoothly into another.

2.4 The Dog's Personality

The character also plays a central role in impulse control and frustration tolerance. Dogs are sensitive to different stimuli. One dog may be a passionate hunter who gets impulse control problems at the sight of a wild animal and has the urge to pounce. The other may ignore all kinds of wild animals but is crazy about playing ball and gradually turns into a ball junkie.

Like humans, dogs also have their likes and dislikes and are more energetic or calm. The character of a dog cannot be changed. Still, through mental exercise and training individually adapted to the dog, you can support your dog by offering the conditions in which his character can develop in the best way possible.

2.5 Bad parenting

Very often (of course not exclusively), a lack of impulse control and a low frustration tolerance result from training mistakes. These usually begin in puppyhood, continue through adolescence and manifest themselves in adulthood. What once may have been cute in a puppy becomes a test of nerves in an adult dog. If the foundation for clear structures and rituals in everyday life isn't laid in puppyhood, you'll likely raise a spoilt dog that hasn't learned clear boundaries. It's neither pleasant for the dog nor you as the owner.

As already mentioned, a dog's personality also significantly establishes impulse control and frustration tolerance. Some relatively easy-going dogs have strong nerves, are calm, and forgive training mistakes. But some dogs tend to be impulsive in character.

These special dogs don't forgive training mistakes and need clear rules and a relatively regular daily routine with the certainty of expectations. In a chaotic environment with ever-changing daily routines, such a dog will not be able to remain happy. The same applies to you as an owner. Of course, this doesn't mean that you shouldn't keep a dog if you lead a varied life. Instead, it means that despite a turbulent life, you can offer the dog a certain degree of stability with places of retreat, adapted training and suitable activities that are part of a holistic growth and approach.

2.6 Health problems

Health problems can lead to a lack of impulse control and low frustration tolerance in your dog. If you're making absolutely no progress in training, the following conditions could be behind it:

- Allergies and itching
  Excruciating itching can be very stressful and make a dog

"fly off the handle". The wrong diet, intolerances and allergies are very unpleasant for your dog and often show themselves in changed behaviour.

- <u>Diseases of the thyroid gland</u>
  If the thyroid gland isn't in balance, it can manifest in mood swings. Consequently, hyperactive behaviour, nervousness, impulsive outbursts, fatigue, depressive moods (the dog is lethargic and wants to sleep a lot), and anxious behaviour may occur.

- <u>Abdominal pain, intestinal inflammation</u>
  Chronic inflammation in the intestines can be a trigger for impulsive behaviour. The feeling of having to defecate and not being able to, or constant diarrhoea, logically strikes a chord.

- <u>Joint pain</u>
  Also, when dogs suffer from joint pain, it often leads to reduced impulse control. It's due to their unwillingness to go for a walk and the constant pain they experience.

Many other diseases can cause a dog's nervous system to become thinner and decrease impulse control and frustration tolerance. So if you notice your dog's behaviour isn't improving or even worsening despite training, go for a check-up at the vet for any undiagnosed diseases. Remember: dogs are true masters at hiding their pain.

2.7 Traumatic Events

Trauma can also seriously lead to an impulse control disorder in dogs and thus to a low frustration tolerance. Dogs suffering from trauma react very strongly to stimuli. What dogs perceive as traumatic depends on individual sensitivity.

Examples of traumatic events:

- Accidents
- Bite attacks from other dogs
- Mistreatment of the owner
- Aversive training
- Neglect
- Loss of home and associated loss of attachment figures
- Bitches abused as birthing machines
- Being caught, etc (applies to dogs from abroad)

All these traumas can lead to anxious and incredibly aggressive behaviour in dogs. Dealing with these dogs is very challenging and the owner needs to apply stress management measures and proper training. The primary goal is to establish a stable environment for these dogs, develop a structured daily routine without excessive demands, and establish a sustainable relationship with their caregiver.

2.7.1 Deprivation Syndrome

A severe form of trauma is deprivation syndrome, a developmental disorder when dogs grow up without social and environmental stimuli. Symptoms of deprivation syndrome are shown when a dog reacts extremely fearfully or aggressively to stimulants.

How does a deprivation syndrome develop?
The best examples of dogs with this syndrome are those bred according to high demand and needs. On the other side, some are kept on a chain in a backyard all their lives. These dogs are shut off

from all stimuli during the essential developmental stages of their lives. They cannot form brain networks that allow them to respond adequately to the environment. Many dogs that come from rescue centres show this behaviour because they mainly were kept alone in a kennel. When they come into our environment, they're massively overstimulated and cannot cope with other people, fellow dogs, cars and the hustle and bustle of the city. The consequences are impulsive and irritable behaviour, which is often acted out in the form of fear and aggression.

Whatever the reason, a dog lacks impulse control and frustration tolerance: With the proper training, it's possible to make up for it even in adult dogs. In the next chapter, you'll learn why positive training is vital for high impulse control and frustration tolerance.

– CHAPTER 3 –

Punishment Vs Reward: When to use What?

T raining dogs with poor impulse control and frustration tolerance must be based on the factors described in the first chapter. These include breed predispositions, character and the ability to cope with stress. It's up to you as the owner to intervene when your dog needs help to manage his stress. Furthermore, you must be aware of what you expect from your dog. Dogs need a clear line, and anything else will only confuse them more. The most important thing is that the training is enjoyable and that you not only focus on the negative characteristics of your dog but appreciate every training progress, no matter how small it is. The type of training plays a significant role in helping your dog establish reasonable impulse control and frustration tolerance.

3.1 Primary and Secondary Reinforcers

In the course of training, it's essential to know what the difference is between primary reinforcers and secondary reinforcers (conditioned reinforcers). **Primary reinforcers** are the (innate) reinforcers that satisfy a dog's basic needs, such as food, sleep, social contact, etc. **Secondary reinforcers** are conditioned, i.e. *learned; involving* a primary reinforcer, such as a treat. Specifically, secondary reinforcers can be a word of praise (marker word), a clicker or a whistle. An example is when a dog is about to run free, and his owner calls him back. As soon as he makes his way back to his owner, he should receive a word of praise (marker word), a click or a whistle (announces the primary reinforcer) followed by a treat or reward. A secondary reinforcer also be a short ball game, running together or even petting.

3.2 Reward and Punishment - Basics

From the point of view of learning theory, there is a between **positive** and **negative punishment**. In positive punishment, an unpleasant stimulus is added, whereas in negative punishment a pleasant stimulus is taken away. A concrete example of **positive punishment** would be when your dog pulls on his lead, and you apply a light pull to make them stop. While a scenario for **negative punishment** would be if your dog jumps up on someone, and that person turns away and ignores him, depriving the dog of attention.

This form of punishment triggers a strong feeling of frustration in a dog. Rewarding a dog immediately for a demonstrated and desired alternative behaviour is very important. An example is when a dog sits down after the person has turned away. Showing this desired behaviour is reinforced by the owner in a high-quality way (using treats or toys, etc.), and the dog will, therefore, most likely show it more often in the future.

> **But be careful:** With **positive** punishment, the cause for which the dog shows this behaviour (pulling on the lead) isn't remedied. The reason for this is that the dog's feelings, which *motivate the dog to* show the behaviour, cannot be made to disappear with punishment. Instead, positive discipline only **suppresses** their behaviour. In the worst case, the aggression or fear builds up, and the situation will escalate sooner or later.

Positive **reinforcement** involves adding something pleasant so that the behaviour shown will occur more often in the future. For example, giving a dog a treat when he walks loosely on the lead. In **negative reinforcement**, a negative stimulus is removed from the dog, giving them a sense of relief. For example, by teaching a dog to "sit" by pushing his rear end to the ground. Removing the added pressure gives the dog a sign of relief.

	Reward	Penalty
Positive	**Adding a pleasant stimulus**	**Adding an unpleasant stimulus**
Example	If a dog is begging at the dining table, a reward is given once they go to their bed and stay there.	A dog is yelled at while beginning at the dining table.
Negative	**Removing an unpleasant stimulus**	**Removing a pleasant Stimulus**
Example	A dog is pushed away when it's begging at the dining table. Once the owner stops pushing them away, the misbehaviour returns.	A dog doesn't receive any attention while beginning at the dining table.

Suitable for a proper education

Not suitable for a proper education

Table 1: Reward vs Punishment

3.2.1 Punishment as a Form of Education

If you want to use punishments in dog training, you must always be aware that:

1. A dog can associate the punishment with their behaviour. For this to happen, the punishment must be given immediately (within one second) after your dog shows certain

behaviour. If you fail to do this, your dog may associate the punishment with something else, leading to further behavioural problems.

2. The punishment must be applied to be strong enough to dissuade the dog from the undesired behaviour.

3. It should be used so that your dog sees no connection between you and the punishment.

If punishment occurs and your dog associates it with you, he will probably show fear and avoidance towards you in the near future. Punishment is not an adequate method in dog training and can even be an animal welfare concern. Punishment shouldn't include any choke collars, electric collars and the likes that are banned in many countries. Shaking cans and other objects, usually thrown to the ground in front of the dog to stop the unwanted behaviour, are also frightening stimuli that can cause lasting damage to trust. Apart from the undesirable consequences of improper, punishment-based training, surely no dog owner wants their relationship with their dog to suffer in this way.

3.2.2 Reward as a Form of Education

Training via positive reinforcement is so much more than just "giving away treats". Specifically, it means adding positivity to your dog's life, triggering a feeling of happiness. Treats and other elements can be used as a reward. By using positive reinforcement, you can encourage your dog to show desired behaviour *more often, more frequently and consistently.*

Although training with positive reinforcement takes a long time, it's the most sustainable way to train dogs. It also builds trust and strengthens the human-dog relationship.

3.2.4 Ideas for positive reinforcement in dog training

To use positive reinforcement correctly in dog training, you should observe your dog well and find out which rewards are of high value to them. The classic treats are a suitable method and easy to use in training. However, some dogs don't like to eat and will not be motivated by food, but might love to play so may be rewarded with games (e.g. tug-of-war or [controlled] ball play). Moreover, environmental rewards (e.g. letting your dog swim if he shows desired behaviour or letting your herding dog observe their environment as a classic eye dog), petting, but also increasing distance if your dog doesn't want contact with other dogs can be rewarding to him.

Preferably, write a list of rewards that are of high quality for your dog and update it regularly. Over time, you'll find more and more reinforcers, and your list will grow longer and longer.

3.3 Clicker Training as a secondary reinforcer

A very good secondary reinforcer used in dog training is the clicker. As already described, a click is a primary reinforcer that satisfies a dog's natural needs, such as food, play, etc. Then there are the secondary reinforcers that announce the primary reinforcers.

By this, the clicker (secondary reinforcer) announces the reward (primary reinforcer) when a dog shows desired behaviour. The advantage of clicker training is that it gives dogs certainty of expectation because the clicker ALWAYS announces a reward. Various clickers make different sounds with some sounding like a children's toy clicker frog; others only make a soft clicking sound.

The disadvantage of a clicker is that you always need to carry it during the training. Furthermore, some dogs may dislike the clicker's sound and are afraid of it.

How is the clicker conditioned?

A quiet, distraction-free, stress-free environment is essential for conditioning the clicker and training your dog. Only then can you and your dog concentrate on the exercises.

The **first step** in clicker training is to condition your dog by rewarding your dog with a treat to eat at the same time as the click. This way, your dog will associate the sound of a clicker with something pleasant. Repeat this exercise until your dog understands the link between the click and the treat.

In the **second step,** your dog should associate the click with the desired behaviour. The best way is to "catch" the behaviour that your dog shows on his own. If your dog spontaneously "sits", a click should follow immediately with the treat. Once he has learned this process, you can start to work practically with the clicker.

If you don't like the clicker and don't want to carry accessories around with you all the time, you can condition your dog to respond to a **marker word.** It's important to choose a word that you rarely or never say in everyday life like "Top". The marker word's structure works like a clicker.

Shaping - Shaping behaviour

Another possibility that you have with the clicker is **shaping** their behaviour. This method requires your dog to think in sections of time. In concrete terms, break down the behaviour you want to "shape" into pieces. This way your dog will learn to arrive at the final result in small steps. Shaping is particularly suitable for teaching dog tricks. But it can also be used in regular training. The unique thing about it is its focus on the method rather than the actual target behaviour and achievement. Because as your dog works out the desired behaviour independently, it becomes more sustainable. Shaping has proven particularly effective with fearful, insecure and susceptible dogs. Since these dogs usually suffer from a lack of self-confidence, working out behaviour on their own is worth its weight in gold because it makes them more confident and is peppered with positive feedback. The disadvantage of shaping is that owners often have to play the long game, as some dogs are slower to learn than others. An example of shaping would be when you want to teach your dog to retrieve an object. The first thing to do is "click" and reward every approach to the object, no matter how small it is. Repeatedly do this until he understands that he should put the object in his mouth and bring it to you. Over time your dog will become more confident and flexible in his thinking. Showing frustration isn't desirable in shaping at the beginning, as some dogs may give up too quickly and thus have negative experiences. Instead, a high reward frequency is good.

Clicker training is an excellent way to train your dog. However, many people prefer using verbal praise to reinforce their dog's behaviour. For this reason, the exercises in this book use praise words. However, you can, of course, also carry out all the activities with the clicker. In the following chapter, you'll learn why impulse-controlled training is necessary and how your dog benefits from it.

– CHAPTER 4 –

Benefits of
Impulse-Controlled Training

I mpulse-controlled training ideally starts when your dog is still a puppy. It begins with ensuring that you don't train them all the time and allow rest periods. Puppies and senior dogs need *at least 22 hours of* sleep a day. An adult dog in its prime also needs *16-20 hours of* sleep. The saying "After tired comes stupid" is justified because if a dog is overtired, he may eventually overcome their tiredness and show restlessness, annoying and exhausting behaviour.

A sleep deficiency can cause a dog to become increasingly nervous and hyper. Yet distinct rest phases are so important that he can process the day's events. Many dog owners make the mistake of immediately reacting and giving in to their dog's demanding behaviour. It can develop into a vicious circle and damage the relationship between "the man and his dog" in the long run.

In **impulse-controlled training,** giving your dog rules and structure is essential. It's also required to "force" your dog to rest when necessary. An example is a dog that follows its owner at every turn. Usually, the motive is that the dog was taught to do this and was unconsciously rewarded for it with "attention". This behaviour is constantly in "expectancy" mode for the dog, which can be very exhausting. If this is your dog's case, the best way to solve this is by not giving him any attention for a while. After some time, he will probably relax and give up chasing. When he's settled down in their place, reward his calm behaviour. Rewarding a calm demeanour should be built into the daily routine.

Your dog voluntarily lies down under your chair in the café and snoozes? **Reward him immediately!** Does he make eye contact with you instead of chasing a deer? **Reward him immediately!** The secret is that dogs very often show desired behaviour BEFORE they start showing undesired behaviour. It can be eye contact or just a slight turn of the head in your direction. The trick is to recognise and reward this behaviour. The advantages of impulse-controlled training are apparent:

- Less stress because their needs are met
- Any hunting or herding instinct becomes controllable
- Your relationship with them improves
- Leash handling improves
- Dog encounters become more relaxed
- Your dog remains manageable and a relaxed everyday companion

Impulse control training is easy to integrate into everyday life. It starts with the slightest changes, for example, feeding, putting on a lead, going into the garden, leaving the house, getting into the car etc. Just by deciding that from that moment on, decisions will be made by you will be impactful Instead of rushing past each other when leaving the house and getting caught up in hustle and stress, the dog can learn to wait until you are ready to leave the door in an orderly manner. There is a saying: 'Strength lies in calmness,' and that is precisely what you should implement in impulse-oriented dog training to achieve a stress-free everyday life with your four-legged friend.

In the next chapter, you'll learn about the essential prerequisites for successful training. The following questions are most frequently asked in dog training practice.

– CHAPTER 5 –

Frequently made Mistakes, and asked Questions

To prepare you for the exercises in this book, here are the most common mistakes and questions about impulse control, frustration tolerance and training.

How do I support my puppy in their impulse control?

The truth is that dogs, by nature, have little to no impulse control, and we as humans have a responsibility to encourage them in this regard. It's essential to teach your dog impulse control as early as possible. Failure to do so may result in him establishing bad habits into adulthood, which will be difficult to control. Teaching a dog impulse control relieves the human-dog team, as it ensures a harmonious everyday life. It's especially beneficial for your dog; as he learns to wait and be patient, his urges for his needs to meet will be reduced. It also reduces stress. Incorporating small impulse control exercises is preferable when your dog is still a puppy. Feeding time is a good time to do this. For example, waiting until your puppy is sitting patiently and only then serving him his food. As he progresses, a command should be introduced to give him the OK to eat.

Can the impulse control of adult dogs be improved?

It's also possible and even recommended to train impulse control in already adult dogs and dogs with a past. The saying "You can't teach an old dog new tricks" is already outdated. The fact is, dogs *always learn* both negative and positive things. If dogs are already showing fearful, aggressive or generally maladaptive behaviour, it's essential to support them. The solution is to adapt training so that it's ideally suited to the dog's age, breed and personality.

Can impulse control in dogs vanish at some point?

You can compare a dog's impulse control to a bank account. If you deposit a lot in the form of training and support, you have a cushion that you can access freely. Impulse control isn't infinite. You can train a dog well, but if there's too much stress in everyday life and the account is never "replenished", their impulse control will also be used up and will eventually be in the minus. You shouldn't expect too much of your dog, and "his account" should always be positive. After a stressful day in the city or training sessions at the dog park, your dog needs rest to process his experiences. It shouldn't be forgotten that adult dogs should rest up to 20 hours daily. If you take your dog to a barbecue or somewhere it's stressful for him, you shouldn't be surprised if he overreacts because his impulse control has been used up.

Why does my dog only show impulse control in certain situations?
Dogs learn according to the *situation* and the place. If you have trained your dog to stay in one place without standing up in the garden, it'll work well in the park. If you now go to a meadow, it'll most likely not work because dogs associate exercise with an environment. The good thing is that the more often you practise with your dog in unfamiliar environments, the faster the *generalisation will* progress, and they'll be able to perform the desired behaviour in other settings, in different contexts and under other distractions.

What does generalisation mean in dog training?
Generalisation suggests that a dog can show a previously learned behaviour always and everywhere. Generalisation works best if you first practise the behaviour in a place with few distractions, with total concentration, and gradually increase the difficulty level. For example, if you now train the "sit" in your quiet living room and the dog has learned and generalised it, the next step is to practise it in your garden and not immediately on a busy main road.

How do I recognise impulse control and frustration tolerance in my dog?

Reasonable impulse control and frustration tolerance in a dog can be recognised by the fact that a dog can sometimes endure certain situations without immediately acting impulsively. It's not possible to give a general explanation of what reasonable impulse control is. Some dogs have balance in all areas of life. However, these dogs are a rarity. Instead, dogs show a lack of impulse control in different areas. One dog may look tiredly at the ball and doesn't want to run after it, while another wants to rush after every moving stimulus. Another dog, on the other hand, pounces on cat excrement lying around at every opportunity, while another would never dream of doing so. As humans, our dogs are also individual and have specific preferences and weak points.

What are the best training conditions?

The best conditions for training impulse control are a balanced atmosphere and a good mood. Training with your dog when stressed, is useless because your attitude will transmit to him. Dogs are true masters at reading their owner's state of mind. Your dog's mood should also be considered because if he is stressed for some reason, in poor health or simply not having a good day, you shouldn't train him. Furthermore, the degree of difficulty of the exercises should be adapted to a dog's level of knowledge and should only be increased step by step.

Training that doesn't exceed **5 to 15 minutes** initially is sufficient for most dogs. Many dogs find the activity strenuous; if you over-work them, you worsen their impulse control rather than improve it. It's also possible to incorporate small impulse control exercises into everyday life. These include making your dog wait a few seconds before giving the OK, for example, before letting him into the garden, putting down his food bowl, or getting him into the car.

Isn't rewarding your dog with a treat the same as bribing him?
Many people ask themselves whether rewarding dogs is equal to bribery. It's answered quite simply: Would you work without receiving a reward? For a dog, training is the same as work; it requires them to concentrate, stay focused and control themselves and thus their natural impulses. The fact that they should be rewarded for these efforts should be self-explanatory. It's also possible to reward your dog in various ways. Environmental rewards such as a short swim, sniffing a particular spot or digging are some great possibilities also.

Do I need to give my dog a treat whenever he shows the desired behaviour?
In principle, a dog should be rewarded for everything they do well because the more often you reinforce desired behaviour, the more it'll be shown. So, it's a win-win for both sides. But - it's like the account I mentioned earlier - the more often you deposit, the more often you can withdraw, as long as you don't slip into the negative. Now, if you're in a situation where you can't reward your dog because, for example, your hands are full of shopping, that shouldn't be a problem and your dog should still show the desired behaviour. Once the desired behaviour is in place, the reward intervals should be increased slightly. Reward him every second or third time he shows the desired behaviour. Vary the reward occasionally. Use a different treat or toy, or praise him. In this way, you prevent your dog from getting into an attitude of expectation. Just make sure that you find the right balance.

In short: Reward as much as possible until the behaviour is correct, and then you can increase the reward intervals a little.

How do I build a good relationship with my dog?
A good relationship is built by giving your dog the feeling that he

can rely on you and that you'll protect him. Furthermore, training together strengthens your bond immensely. Giving your dog enough rest periods is just as much a part of this as allowing adventure walks and activities that he likes to do. Rules and rituals in everyday life give the dog security. Playing together is fun, and reading and interpreting his body language settles many conflicts in advance.

How do I know that my dog is overwhelmed?

As discussed, overstrained dogs show (several) stress signals. Perhaps, they cannot calm down and become more sensitive to stimuli. Massive stress additionally sharpens a dog's senses, which is why impulsive reactions occur. In training, you can recognise that your dog is overworked by becoming increasingly unfocused and generally appearing demotivated. It is important to interrupt the situation and practice stress management when you notice that the dog is overwhelmed.

What does stress management mean in dog training?

Stress management in dog training means interpreting the dog's signs of stress and reacting accordingly. An example of this is creating a distance from the trigger: If your dog reacts fearfully to cyclists, have a stress-reducing effect by moving him away from the trigger, in the best case, already when you notice the first stress signals. Doing this prevents escalation and supports your dog's needs. Giving your dog a routine, observing the individual distance, and sufficient mental training are all part of stress management.

Now that you know all the basics for successful impulse-controlled training, let's get started with the practice in the next chapter.

Have fun training!

– CHAPTER 6 –

Impulse Control And Frustration Tolerance Training

The training for impulse control and frustration tolerance is best started in puppyhood. The exercises in this book are suitable for preventing and correcting impulse control disorders.

The **124 exercises** presented in this book range from simple basics that you can use to promote impulse control from day one. These workouts will work as a miracle in activities that can be used with dogs with impulse control disorder. It's impossible to offer step-by-step exercises for some behavioural problems or training mistakes. Instead, you'll find recommendations on the best ways to correct the problem. Following the impulse control exercises, you'll find a bonus chapter with **21 activity ideas** for the perfect workout for your dog.

6.1 Basic Exercises for Self-control and Obedience

This chapter describes exercises you should teach your dog from an early age to strengthen his impulse control and frustration tolerance playfully and cooperatively. By supporting your puppy or young dog with exercises for high impulse control, the likelihood of behavioural problems as an adult dog will decrease immensely. Here is a hint about rewarding treats: Taking treats out of the daily food ration is advisable to avoid overfeeding. You should hold the treat between your index finger and thumb and hand it to your dog. Allowing him to lick the treat from the palm of your hand may lead to the treat falling on the floor and your dog's concentration being lost for a short time.

As a quick reminder, here's a tip about rewarding exercises that your dog has largely understood:
To avoid your dog expecting a treat every time, vary the reward

with something else, such as a toy or a sniff break, and increase the reward intervals. So, he only receives something special every third or fifth time. You can apply this principle to almost all exercises except for "recall". The latter must also work in emergencies.

🐶 EXERCISE 1 🐶
"Well Done" – Command Conditioning (indoor/outdoor)

The first and most important command you should train your dog to do is the "well done" command, a positive command that confirms to him that they've done the right thing and increases the possibility that he will repeat this behaviour. It also encourages concentration and eye contact, two critical aspects of training. Pick a single word. "Great", "Super", and "Fine" are among the most typical. Choose a word you don't use too often because it's a promise in exchange for a treat, even if it slips.

Step 1: Kneel in front of your dog and take nine treats in your hand.

Step 2: Give your dog each treat in turn. Make sure you first say the command, e.g. "Great", wait for half a second and then grab his paw with your other hand.

Step 3: Repeat steps 1 and 2 for 2 - 3 days approx. 10 to 12 times a day leaving at least 20 minutes between repetitions. You're welcome to do another exercise during this time. However, continue to consistently use the command.

Step 4: Finally, test out the success of the training by standing with your back about 5 - 10 m away from your dog at a randomly selected time and outside of a training session. Say the command softly. If he responds, the training is booming and they should be **rewarded** him **again**.

Addition for advanced learners: If he already knows the "well done" command, you can increase the difficulty level by, for example, applying the command to him from a distance when you see that he's done something particularly well. A possible scenario could be that he's resisted running after an object or that another goal that you've been working on together has been reached. Immediately apply the command and reward your dog.

Exercise objective: Your dog is conditioned to a single word of praise. This way, you have him under control faster and better. Timing is the key.

6.1.1 Basic obedience exercises "sit" and "down"

At any age, you should teach your dog basic obedience. The following exercises describe their structure.

🐶 EXERCISE 2 🐶
Set up the command "sit"
(Indoor/Outdoor)

Mastering the command "sit" is important. It's one of the first commands that puppies should learn. It's so helpful for you as it can be used universally and extended later.

Step 1: Stand in front of your dog with a treat.

Step 2: Hold the treat above his head and slowly guide it backwards.

Step 3: Give him the treat as soon as he sits down.

Step 4: Later on, just before your dog sits, say the command "sit". By doing this, he associates the word directly with the activity.

Addition for advanced learners: If your dog has already learned the command, start giving it to him in various places. You can also gradually increase the level of distraction. In this way, he will generalize the command and use it safely in every situation.

Exercise objective: Your dog is trained in the command "sit".

🐶 EXERCISE 3 🐶
Capture the command "sit"
(Indoor/Outdoor)

Sometimes you can also try the command "sit". This method is perfect for dogs that like to sit often anyway. Since the dog offers to "sit" on its own, the dog will rapidly associate the command with the activity.

Step 1: Watch your dog carefully and have treats ready.

Step 2: As soon as he sits down, praise him and give him a treat.

Step 3: If he shows the sit command more often, introduce the word signal and, if possible, give it before you see that he wants to sit.

Addition for advanced learners: You have often rewarded the spontaneous sitting of the dog and would like to introduce a command for it. When you see that your dog wants to sit, say the command first and then reward him. He will quickly associate the command with sitting.

Exercise objective: Your dog sits more often spontaneously, calmly and without the command "sit".

🐶 EXERCISE 4 🐶
Set up the command "down" by luring (indoor/outdoor)

Step 1: You have the treat in your closed hand and place it on the floor in front of your dog, still holding it in your hand.

Step 2: When he sniffs it, slowly withdraw your hand and he should now lie down.

Step 3: When he's in place, give him the treat.

Step 4: When he has learned "down", start saying "down" before he lies down.

Note: Luring is a good way of teaching your dog certain things, as long as you then - when he's mastered the command - weed it out again so that only the actual command, in this case, "down", is carried out.

Addition for advanced learners: When your dog has associated the "down" command with the activity, you can leave out the hand movement and apply the command and reward afterwards.

Exercise objective: Your dog learns to lie down on command.

🐶 EXERCISE 5 🐶
Set up the command "down" through luring 2 (Indoor/Outdoor)

Another helpful exercise to build up the "down" command with a lure is to allow him to smell the treat and follow it.

Step 1: Hold the treat in your hand and let him smell it.

Step 2: Pull the treat close to his chest towards the floor and stay in this position.

Step 3: Now wait until he's lying down and then reward him with the treat immediately.

Addition for advanced learners: If your dog can link the command "down" with the activity, you can leave out the hand movement and apply the command and reward afterwards.

Exercise objective: Your dog learns to lie down on command.

🐶 EXERCISE 6 🐶
Capture the command "down"
(Indoor/Outdoor)

A good way to teach your dog the command "down" is to capture it. This method's advantage is that it strengthens a dog's self-esteem because it teaches them the command independently.

Step 1: Watch your dog carefully.

Step 2: As soon as he spontaneously goes "down", reward him.

Step 3: If he goes "down" more often, introduce the command, preferably when you notice that he wants to lie down.

Step 4: Increase the duration: If he is good and stays in the square, move back; if he stays in the garden, go to him and reward him. Slowly increase the amount of time your dog stays in the square. Continue to increase the distance to them gradually.

Addition for advanced learners: You have already rewarded your dog's spontaneous lying down many times and would like to introduce a command for it. When you see that your dog wants to lie down, say the command first and then reward him. This way he'll quickly associate the command with lying down.

Exercise objective: Your dog learns "down" and should remain there even if you move away.

🐶 EXERCISE 7 🐶
Capture the command "down"
Teaching the dog to stop
(Indoor/Outdoor)

The command "stop" can be used well to make your dog stop in action. For example, in the situation when your dog is off the lead and running around free and you want to put his lead back on.

Step 1: Say "stop" with his lead on and remain rooted to the spot.

Step 2: When he stops, reward immediately at the level of his nose so that he doesn't sit down.

Step 3: When he reacts well on the lead, vary the exercise and continue, for example, with a dragline. Later, practise the command standing without a lead.

Addition for advanced learners: When your dog has already learned the command "stop", it's a matter of generalizing the exercise and applying it in many different places and scenarios.

Exercise objective: Your dog learns to stop on command.

🐶 EXERCISE 8 🐶
Teaching the dog "Stay"
(Indoor/Outdoor)

Usually, a dog should always wait for the release command during all exercises. However, if this hasn't been taught correctly, train the command "stay".

Step 1: For example, if your dog is lying down, give him the command "Stay" and move back. If he remains lying down, take a step forward and reward him. Be careful how you reward him so he's not tempted to get up.

Step 2: Take a step back and approach and reward him after a few seconds.

Step 3: Repeat the 2nd step and gradually increase the distance. In addition, keep increasing the duration that you return to your dog.

Addition for advanced learners: When your dog has mastered the command "stay" quite well, slowly make the exercise more difficult by commanding him to "stay" and, for example, walk out of sight.

Exercise objective: Your dog learns to stay down until you give him the go-ahead.

6.1.2 Eye contact

The first eye contact exercises should always be in a low-distraction environment, preferably indoors. After that, you can train the practices both indoors and outdoors. Eye contact is crucial in building and maintaining a good relationship between humans and dogs. Intense eye contact releases the bonding hormone oxytocin which strengthens the bond. If you encourage eye contact at an early age and reward your dog repeatedly, he'll stay connected and close to you even during puberty and eventually grow into a relaxed dog in adulthood.

🐶 EXERCISE 9 🐶
Promote eye contact
(indoor/outdoor)

Encouraging eye contact can take your relationship with your dog to the next level.

Step 1: Take a good quality treat in each hand.

Step 2: Command your dog to sit down.

Step 3: Stretch both arms away from you to the side. In this situation, most dogs will look at the hands because they can figure out that's where the treat is. But the key is to be a little patient until they realise that they should look at you. It's vital that you remain calm and don't say anything at this moment.

Step 4: As soon as your dog looks at you, give him the treat from one of your hands.

Addition for advanced learners: If your dog makes eye contact with you now and then, you can occasionally reward him for it. This way, he'll intensify the eye contact.

Exercise objective: To develop your dog's concentration through eye contact and build that important bond. This exercise can also be trained well with dogs that are very fixated on their ball. Simply replace the treat in your hands with a toy.

🐶 EXERCISE 10 🐶
Promoting eye contact while playing (Indoor/Outdoor)

Dogs love to play, so what could be more natural than encouraging eye contact through play?

Step 1: Squat or stand with your dog on the floor for this exercise. Prepare small treats and place one of them on the floor.

Step 2: When your dog approaches the treat, say *no* and cover the treat with your foot or hand.

Step 3: As soon as he looks at you, release the treat.

Addition for advanced learners: If your dog is already looking at you of his own accord, you no longer need to cover the treat but can give them a command to release it.

Exercise objective: Your dog learns to talk to you through eye contact.

🐶 EXERCISE 11 🐶
Encourage eye contact with another person (indoor/outdoor)

Step 1: Give the treats to another person so your dog sees them.

Step 2: Stand side by side with the other person.

Step 3: As soon as your dog takes his eyes off the other person and looks directly at you, the other person may give him the treat.

Addition for advanced dog learners: If your dog has already fig-ured out that he must look at you to receive something pleasant, the person can vary the way they give the treat by maybe playfully throwing it to him, etc. This way, the situation becomes a fun game for your dog.

Exercise objective: This activity is designed to reinforce the bond between you and your dog. First, he learns that he must first con-sult with you through eye contact before accepting anything from strangers.

🐶 EXERCISE 12 🐶
Reward spontaneous eye contact (Indoor/Outdoor)

If your dog shows spontaneous eye contact in various situations, this makes living together much easier because he automatically consults you.

Step 1: Take treats with you wherever you go with him.

Step 2: If your dog is busy, perhaps sniffing or walking loosely on his lead, and then looks at you, reward him.

Note: If your dog rarely shows spontaneous eye contact, vary the reward intervals to avoid expectations.

Exercise objective: To reinforce eye contact and increase the fre-quency of spontaneous responses from your dog. This way, he learns that it's worthwhile to always be in contact with you.

🐶 EXERCISE 13 🐶
Eye contact before food release
(Indoor)

Demanding eye contact before giving food trains your dog's impulse control very well and keeps him responsive.

Step 1: Command him to sit down and wait until he's sitting patiently.

Step 2: Place the food bowl quietly in front of him.

Step 3: Wait until he's no longer looking at the food but at you.

Step 4: As soon as he's made eye contact with you, give him the signal to eat.

Exercise objective: To train your dog to refrain from going to his bowl while you're filling it. But instead, wait for your signal. By doing this, you are strengthening impulse control concerning food at an early age.

🐶 EXERCISE 14 🐶
Approved Eye contact (advanced)
(Indoor/Outdoor)

This exercise is a good preparation for later training. Your dog shouldn't pick up anything from the ground.

Step 1: Command your dog to sit.

Step 2: Place a treat on the floor in front of him and command him to "wait".

Step 3: Wait until he's looking at you, and then command that he's allowed to take the treat.

Exercise objective: **To train your** dog to interact with you before picking something up from the floor.

🐶 EXERCISE 15 🐶
Impulse control for advanced learners (Indoor/Outdoor)

This exercise is suitable for advanced dogs who have already mastered the previous exercises perfectly:

Step 1: Command your dog to lie "down".

Step 2: Put some treats on his paws.

Step 3: As soon as he looks at you, give the signal and let him eat the treat from his paws.

Exercise objective: To strengthen impulse control and consolidate eye contact generally.

6.1.3 Promoting attention - exercises for impulse control and frustration tolerance

The following exercises are perfect for strengthening your dog's concentration. Furthermore, they ensure reasonable impulse control and frustration tolerance. Everyday life is very suitable for incorporating practices when your dog has to show a lot of self-control. Attention and concentration exercises take a toll on a dog's mind and make them tired, but they can pursue their canine abilities and be themselves.

🐶 EXERCISE 16 🐶
Rewarding concentration
(indoor/outdoor)

This exercise encourages your dog to concentrate on you. A second person is required. If you exercise outdoors, your dog should be in an enclosed area, or secured to a dragline.

Step 1: Command him to lie down in a specific "place".

Step 2: The second person should now try to distract him (with a treat or a ball) and keep walking past you. If your dog remains calm in the square, keep rewarding him for it. Make sure you hand him the treat, in a way that he's not tempted to get up.

Step 3: If he's able to remain calm during this exercise, it's time to reward him with a high-quality reward.

Addition for advanced learners: This difficulty level of the exercise can be increased by allowing the second person to run past quickly and perhaps call out to add a degree of distraction. By doing this, your dog will be more challenged to control his impulses.

Exercise Objective: Your dog gives you full attention and does not get distracted by anyone else.

🐶 EXERCISE 17 🐶
10 treats game
(indoor/outdoor)

This game is ideal for promoting a dog's impulse control and strengthening the bond between you and your dog.

Step 1: Take ten treats and put them in a bowl.

Step 2: Then call your dog to you. Now say out loud "one" and put the first treat in your hand. Do this with all the treats, counting up to ten. If your dog is still young, he may become very restless while you're counting the pieces of food. In this case, don't count to ten, but only to three. It's important that your dog remains calm because it's an exercise to strengthen impulse control.

Step 3: When you have counted the treats, say "1" and give him the first treat. Once he's finished chewing and remained focused, continue with the other treats. To make it more playful, throw the pieces of food challenging him to search for them.

Exercise objective: Your dog takes a step back during the count and gives you his total concentration.

🐶 EXERCISE 18 🐶
Concentration promotion and utilisation
(Indoor/Outdoor)

This game is good for keeping your dog busy and challenging him to his nose intensively.

Step 1: Find a muffin baking tin or an egg box.

Step 2: Put treats in each part of the baking tin or egg box and place a tennis ball on top. Socks are also perfect for hiding the treat or food.

Step 3: Command your dog to sit and place the tin or egg box on the floor. Then give him the signal or call so that he can now begin his search.

Addition for advanced learners: You can increase the difficulty level by putting treats only in every second 'hole' of the tin. But be careful! Don't set the difficulty level too high initially because this exercise promotes frustration tolerance.

Exercise objective: Your dog uses his nose and paws to find the treats, encouraging mental exercise.

🐶 EXERCISE 19 🐶
Hide and Seek game
(Outdoor)

This exercise can be done outside. It's a simple game that you can do repeatedly on your walk. Go into the forest with your dog armed with lots of treats and find a suitable tree.

Step 1: Command your dog to sit.

Step 2: Hide the pieces of food up in the tree. Use the bark of the tree for this.

Step 3: Give your dog the OK to search when you have finished hiding the treats.

Addition for advanced learners: To strengthen your dog's coordination, you can try to place the treats in the tree so that he has to stretch further and further to reach them.

Exercise objective: So that your dog's self-control is trained to wait until you have hidden the treats. Furthermore, he's kept mentally occupied while searching for them.

🐶 EXERCISE 20 🐶
Encourage the dog to rest
(Indoor)

This exercise teaches your dog to be calm and that they aren't always the centre of attention.

Step 1: If your dog uses vocalisations, such as barking or whining, to get attention, ignore him until he's quiet and maybe even lying down.

Step 2: When he's calmed down, reward him with praise or petting. However, be careful not to get him overexcited again by praising him too much.

Addition for advanced learners: It's also helpful to gradually increase the reward intervals as soon as he masters this exercise. In this way, you avoid keeping your dog in a constant, expectant state.

Exercise objective: Your dog learns that he can't be entertained all day. It takes the stress out of the situation and allows him to relax.

This exercise can be easily incorporated into the daily routine. So when you see your dog resting and relaxing, reward him.

🐶 EXERCISE 21 🐶
Impulse control on the ball
(Indoor/Outdoor)

Use your favourite ball for this exercise or your dog's favourite toy.

Step 1: Command your dog to sit.

Step 2: Throw them their ball.

Step 3: Signal to them to retrieve the ball and play with it. If he immediately chases the ball before you've signalled the release, keep him on a lead so that he doesn't catch the ball and feel successful.

Addition for advanced learners: When he has learned on the lead that he only gets to the object after permission is given, you can train the exercise without a lead.

Exercise objective: Your dog learns to resist moving stimuli and refrains from chasing.

6.1.4 Start and stop commands

The purpose of start and stop commands is to make a dog stop what they're doing. The important thing with these commands is that they're well-conditioned and built up positively. When a dog masters these commands, you can control them much better. Furthermore, "start" and "stop" helps interrupt unwanted behaviour, such as when they want to pick up something unknown off the ground.

🐶 EXERCISE 22 🐶
Break up and stop command during play (indoor/outdoor)

Step 1: Sit on the floor with your dog's favourite toy and play together at first.

Step 2: Then, after a while take the toy and hide it behind your back. Encourage your dog to move back a few steps.

Step 3: Remove the toy from behind your back, but as you do block it from the dog's sight and say "no".

Step 4: Only once you say the release command, such as "OK" should the toy be returned to him.

Exercise objective: Your dog learns not to claim his toy or snatch it out of yours or someone else's hand, for example, children.

This exercise can also be performed with treats.

🐶 EXERCISE 23 🐶
Stop command "No" - conditioning (Indoor)

The stop command is very important in dog training and can be used universally in everyday life. It can prevent many unpleasant situations.

Step 1: Call your dog to you and place a treat in your open hand.

Step 2: Use the command "OK", to allow your dog to take a treat. Repeat these three to four times.

Step 3: Now, put a treat in your hand again, but instead of saying OK, say "no" and close your hand into a fist. At this point, many dogs may start to scratch at the hand to try to open it. But wait until he's calm.

Step 4: As soon as he's calm, command that he can take the treat from your open hand.

Exercise objective: The stop command "No" is established playfully.

Note that giving the "OK" command is essential before opening your hand. Otherwise, your dog may interpret the opening of the hand as the actual command.

🐶 EXERCISE 24 🐶
Strengthen stop command – Advanced (Indoor)

Step 1: Proceed in the same way as in exercise 23, except that you no longer close your hand when you say "no". This checks whether your dog has been conditioned correctly to the stop command.

Step 2: Use the stop command "no" and present the treat to him with an open hand.

Step 3: If your dog now keeps distance and shows no ambition to take the treat, give him a treat from the OTHER hand.

In this situation, where he's not kept their distance and tried to get the treat, close your hand so that he doesn't feel a sense of achievement.

Exercise objective: On the one hand, the stop command is generalised, and on the other hand, it's used to check to what extent your dog has understood the stop command.

🐾 EXERCISE 25 🐾
Break-off signal for advanced
(Indoor)

Step 1: Sit on a chair or stand with lots of small treats.

Step 2: Start throwing the treats on the floor and give your dog the OK to retrieve the pieces of food. Repeat this process three to four times.

Step 3: Now throw a treat on the floor, say "no", and cover it with your foot. When your dog keeps his distance, give him a treat from your other hand and retrieve the treat from the floor. In this exercise, it's easier if you keep the treat close to you on the floor so you can reach it.

Addition for advanced learners: If your dog keeps his distance from the treat on the floor when you say "no", you don't need to cover it and you can feed him directly from the other hand.

Exercise objective: To strengthen the stop command.

🐾 EXERCISE 26 🐾
Generalise the break-off signal
(Outdoor)

The generalisation of the exercise is very important so your dog can apply what he's learned in other places.

Step 1: Take your dog into the garden or another place with few distractions.

Step 2: Start putting treats in the garden/place while your dog is waiting in the house or car. They shouldn't be watching you. The treats shouldn't be as high quality as the indoor exercises. However, it would help if you had high-quality treats in your pocket for your dog's reward.

Step 3: Get your dog and walk him past the treat. When he discovers the treats, say "no". But when he turns to you, reward him with your high-quality treat. However, if he's more interested in the goodies on the ground, stand still and don't allow him to retrieve them. Please wait until he turns to you, and only then reward him.

Addition for advanced learners: Once your dog has understood the exercise in familiar surroundings, practice in busier places, for example, an unfamiliar meadow or a quiet car park.

Exercise objective: Your dog learns not to pick up anything from the floor and leave an object on command.

🐶 EXERCISE 27 🐶
Breaking playtime
(indoor/outdoor)

Puppies, in particular, tend to overdo it when playing and can become quite rough. This exercise teaches you how to give puppies a time-out.

Step 1: Start playing with your puppy.

Step 2: If your puppy gets too rough, stop playing and ignore him. If he doesn't stop chasing you, leave the room and only return when he's calmed down.

Step 3: When you return, praise him vocally and continue the game.

Exercise objective: Your puppy learns that the game will be stopped if he gets too rough.

This exercise is also suitable for puppies who like jumping up or testing their bite inhibition on parts of your body.

6.2 Housetraining Exercises

Puppies cannot hold urine or faeces during the first months of their life. It's not until 14-16 weeks of age that they begin to control their excretory organs. A simple rule of thumb when it comes to "house-training" a puppy is about two hours per month of life. Housetraining a puppy is a challenging task and requires patience, perseverance and time. Even adult dogs are sometimes not house-trained for a variety of reasons. If this is the case, proceed with using the same exercises with your adult dog as you would a puppy. It can also happen that a puppy needs to go to the toilet at night. In this case, encouraging them to use a crate is a good idea. This way you know when they want to go out. Getting accustomed to a crate can also be helpful later on, for example when a lively young dog needs to calm down. It can also serve as a secure place for the dog when, for instance, the visitor's presence becomes overwhelming

🐶 EXERCISE 28 🐶
Housetraining for puppies
(Indoor/Outdoor)

With this exercise, you'll quickly get your puppy house-trained. However, it requires impeccable observation skills.

Step 1: Assign your puppy a place outside where he can go to the toilet in the future. This is advantageous so he knows immediately and won't take time searching for a suitable place in the future.

Step 2: Keep a close eye on your puppy. If he tries to relieve himself inside, pick him up and take him outside.

Step 3: When he's finished "doing his business", it's time to acknowledge this lavishly with praise and treats.

Furthermore, you can say a word, for example, "wee-wee", just before he does his business. This ensures that he associates the word "wee-wee" with the impulse to urinate, and you can already command it.

Exercise objective: Your puppy will be house-trained quickly.

If a mishap does occur, wipe it away without comment. Never scold your puppy if he goes to the toilet inside but train your powers of observation. In the future, he might secretly go to a spot in the house out of fear. In addition, puppies don't yet have very mature sphincters and therefore have to do their business more often.

🐶 EXERCISE 29 🐶
Crate training
(Indoor)

Crate training for puppies has been very successful because the puppy has to announce when he needs to go.

Step 1: Place the crate in a suitable place. Condition your puppy positively by putting something tasty inside.

Step 2: For positive conditioning, always throw a treat into the box when walking by.

Step 3: Start by introducing the command, for example, "box". Say the command as soon as he starts walking towards the crate. The crate shouldn't be closed at the beginning of the training.

Step 4: When he goes in voluntarily, you can start closing it for a few seconds. Once he's relaxed inside, give him a treat THROUGH the bars.

Step 5: In this step, gradually and slowly move away from the crate.

Step 6: Now, slowly increase the time the crate is closed.

Exercise objective: To use the crate as a place of retreat. Note: Using the crate is a controversial issue. Should the door be left open or not? There are different opinions on this. However, a dog should never be locked in a box for hours on end, but they should only serve as a positively constructed safe place of retreat.

6.2.1 Urination Exercises

If a dog suddenly urinates inside the home, there can be various reasons behind it. If medical reasons are ruled out, it can be assumed that a mental problem is the cause. Reasons for sudden urination can be severe changes in the everyday life of the human-dog team, e.g. a move, the loss of a caregiver, great grief or jealousy. But also traumatic events, abuse or stress can lead to uncleanliness. Another reason can be the longing for attention. The common problem is that urinating when greeted is misunderstood as an expression of joy, but it's an expression of *stress* and *excitement.* Too short walks and little mental and physical exercise can also cause dogs to become unhouse-trained or urinate in the home and other inappropriate places.

🐶 EXERCISE 30 🐶
Urinating upon greeting
(Indoor)

When dogs suffer from separation anxiety, they can become un-
clean. Fear and stress lead them to no longer be able to control
their urination. An excited greeting ritual when coming home also
encourages this behaviour. It's often mistaken for joy but is actually
a sign of insecurity.

Step 1: When you come home, greet your dog in a relaxed
and calm manner.

Step 2: Don't encourage hyperactive behaviour when greeting. If your dog jumps up at you, whines or howls, ignore him
and turn away. Don't greet him until he's calmed down.

Exercise objective: Your dog learns that your return is normal and
not an unusual occurrence.

Tip: If your dog doesn't calm down when you return home, despite
trying to ignore him, you can put him on the lead and take him to
his place. Wait there until he's calmed down. Most dogs will lie
down after a few minutes. Alternatively, when you come home,
you can immediately try to put them on their leash and take them
for a short walk. It'll teach them to urinate exclusively outside
again.

Tip: Urination due to separation anxiety/stress Sometimes dogs
aren't housetrained because they suffer from massive separation
anxiety. This problem needs to be tackled at the root. Detailed
exercises to help the dog with separation anxiety and stress can be
found in chapter 6.6.1. separation anxiety.

6.2.2 Exercises on marking behaviour

Marking is a natural behaviour among dogs and serves the purpose of communication. But quadrupeds mark out various impulses, such as stress, territorial behaviour, and gestures of humility or excitement. It's important to note that not only male dogs mark. If your dog marks excessively outdoors, you must do something about it.

🐶 EXERCISE 31 🐶
Intensive marking behaviour
(Outdoor)

Many dogs tend to mark excessively. It should be counteracted at a young age, as soon as the male dog begins to scratch. But you can also break adult dogs' habit of unwanted marking with the help of the stop command.

Step 1: Establish an abort command (see further in chapter section 6.1.4 Start and abort commands)

Step 2: If your dog is used to the stop command, use this in the case of unwanted marking behaviour. Using this command when he looks at you is your best chance.

Step 3: As soon as he gives you his attention, reward him with high-quality treats.

Exercise objective: Your dog learns not to mark excessively so that car tyres, house walls etc., remain free of urine.

Tip: If your dog marks at strangers' homes, it's advisable to keep him on a lead when visiting. Take his blanket with you and give him the command to "lie down". This way, he can lie relaxed beside you, and no marking can occur in a stranger's home.

🐾 EXERCISE 32 🐾
Blanket training
(Indoor/Outdoor)

Blanket training is helpful if a dog can relax anytime, even in unfamiliar places. For this, you need a blanket and treats.

Step 1: Spread out the blanket, lead your dog to his blanket and wait until he lies down. He should lie down without a command from you.

Step 2: Once he's lying on the blanket, praise him calmly and reward him with a treat. He should remain lying down until you give him a signal.

Step 3: When he's gained an understanding that he should remain laid down, introduce a command, for example, "blanket", when he begins to wander over to it.

Exercise objective: Blanket training is advantageous as dogs generally warm immediately to a blanket. By doing this exercise, your dog not only can go with you wherever you go but also has a safe place to relax.

6.3 Feeding behaviour

Food aggression is a widespread phenomenon among dogs. One possible cause may be that a dog has had previous experiences of someone taking their food away or being disturbed while eating. A dog's primary motivation to defend its food is the impulse of fear. It's best to start training dogs from an early age so that they don't develop any aggressive behaviour towards food. However, some dogs may not be able to eat peacefully but have not established this aggression involving food. In this case, they show a hectic and nervous eating style for no reason. The opposite case can also occur frequently, i.e. dogs that don't want to eat.

🐶 EXERCISE 33 🐶
Prevent food aggression
(Indoor)

The exercise is suitable for training impulse control concerning food and preventing food aggression. In the beginning, it's good to train under low-distraction conditions. You'll need high-quality treats for this.

Step 1: Prepare your dog's food bowl and give him the command to sit. Make sure he's relaxed as possible.

Step 2: Place the food bowl in front of him and give him the command to eat.

Step 3: Sit on the floor facing your dog, take the bowl, put a treat in it and give it back to them.

Addition for advanced learners: With time, you can add slight distractions. For example, have another person walk by the bowl while you hand it to your dog.

Exercise objective: Your dog positively associates removing his bowl as he gets something better in return.

Caution! Please don't do this exercise if your dog is already showing threatening behaviour and you risk being bitten. This exercise is only for the prevention of food aggression.

🐶 EXERCISE 34 🐶
Swaps and "Drop"
(Indoor/Outdoor)

This exercise can be easily incorporated into everyday life. A dog needs to learn that it's worthwhile to exchange its resources.

Step 1: In this scenario, your dog is chewing on a bone.

Step 2: Show him, nearby, a high-quality treat or a desirable toy.

Step 3: As soon as he opens his mouth to make the exchange, say the command "drop".

Step 4: Give him the alternative object and repeat steps 3 and 4 regularly until he associates the command with opening his mouth.

Addition for advanced learners: If your dog allows bartering in a low-distraction environment, you can start doing the exercise in strange places so he learns that bartering can take place anywhere, not just at home. This exercise supports, among others, exercise 40, "Eating from the street floor".

Exercise objective: Your dog learns to give up desirable objects voluntarily in the future because he knows that he'll receive something of higher value in return.

🐶 EXERCISE 35 🐶
Food aggression with fear
(Indoor)

Some dogs show fear of aggressive behaviour concerning eating. Only do this exercise if your dog doesn't show any threatening behaviour!

Step 1: Practise how to approach your dog's food bowl as a human. At first, stand quietly at a great distance and wait until he has reached the bowl. As time goes by, approach the bowl very carefully. Walk in an arc because dogs perceive direct and frontal approaches as a possible threat.

Step 2: Fill only part of his daily food into the bowl. Then wait until he's finished eating before taking it and serving him another small portion.

Step 3: Teach him that placing your hand close to the bowl while there's still food in it is normal. While he's eating, continue throwing a treat into his bowl.

Exercise objective: Your anxious dog learns that it's not necessary to inhale his food when stressed.

Tip: Food aggression with threatening behaviour
Training dogs that already show threatening behaviour when approaching the bowl is the same as with fearful dogs. BUT - under no circumstances should the bowl be taken away from an aggressive dog while they are still eating, as this can make it even more valuable to them and lead them to react more aggressively. In the worst case, it will intensify food aggression. Furthermore, you should proceed gently and gradually when approaching with your hand. Ideally, it would help to throw the treats into the bowl from a great

distance and slowly increase the training.

Tip: For dogs that gobble

As a management measure, it has proven beneficial to use an anti-gobbling bowl to protect a dog's stomach and intestines. In the long run, however, this behaviour should be trained away. The cause often lies in a dog's puppyhood, namely when the breeder forced them to eat from a bowl and thus had to virtually fight for food.

🐶 EXERCISE 36 🐶
Playfully vary feeding times
(Outdoor)

This exercise is well suited for dogs that are both very fixated on feeding times and immediately go into frenzied behaviour at the sighting of food.

Step 1: Don't feed your dog from the bowl for a while, but give him food on the walk. Let him look for it, e.g. in the forest.

Step 2: Give him a "sit" signal and hide his food in a tree trunk.

Step 3: Give him the OK to search for the food. Help him a little if this game is still new to him.

Exercise objective: Take the stress out of feeding by varying the feeding times. At the same time, encourage him to use his nose intensively to keep him mentally busy.

🐶 EXERCISE 37 🐶
The dog doesn't want to eat
(Indoor)

Many dogs don't like to eat. Under no circumstances should you force them to eat or spoil it by offering different meals repeatedly in the hope that they'll pick one of them. It can unnecessarily increase a dog's insecurity about food.

Step 1: Ignore your dog while you prepare his food.

Step 2: Place the bowl on the floor without comment and move away.

Step 3: Make sure you continue ignoring him while he's eating. If he hasn't touched his bowl after about half an hour, take it away without comment and put it down again a few hours later.

Exercise objective: To remove pressure and uncertainty from your dog during feeding.

🐶 EXERCISE 38 🐶
Breaking the begging habit at the table
(Indoor/Outdoor)

In most cases, begging for food from the table is a learned behaviour that has been reinforced repeatedly.

Step 1: In this scenario, you're eating something and your dog starts begging.

Step 2: Lead your dog to his place and encourage him to lie down.

Step 3: If he remains well-behaved, place a treat in his bowl in ten seconds intervals.

Step 4: Increase the time interval between rewards more and more.

Exercise objective: Your dog always goes to his seat when you eat something.

Tip - Ignore begging: If your dog starts begging during mealtime, ignore it. If he demands your attention by scratching or whining, continue to ignore it. You must remain consistent here because your dog should no longer feel a sense of achievement when begging.

🐶 EXERCISE 39 🐶
Break the habit of stealing food (Indoor/Outdoor)

There are different reasons why dogs steal (especially food). Most of the time, stealing is a learned behaviour when dogs are allowed to beg at the table.

Step 1: Put your food on the table and leave the room.

Step 2: Observe your dog unobtrusively from a distance.

Step 3: As soon as he shows an attempt to eat the food, enter the room and send him to his seat.

Step 4: If he stays in his place, reward him accordingly.

Exercise objective: Your dog learns not to steal anything from the table. Support this exercise by additionally ignoring him if he's begging at the table. Your friends and acquaintances should also follow this and not encourage any begging at the table.

🐾 EXERCISE 40 🐾
Breaking the habit of eating off of the street (Indoor/Outdoor)

Some dogs eat all kinds of things from the street; this can be rubbish, excrement or other items. For this exercise, your dog must know the stop command (chapter 6.1.4 in this book).

Step 1: As soon as you see your dog walking towards something on the street floor, tighten his lead so they're not able to reach it.

Step 2: Now use the command stop, e.g. "No". When he turns to you, reward him immediately.

Exercise objective: Your dog no longer picks up objects from the floor. Only extend the training to an outdoor area once he reliably shows the desired behaviour indoors.

Note: Exercise 34 (Swaps and "drop") supports this exercise objective.

6.4 Leash Handling

There are many reasons dogs cannot walk on a lead. Most of the time, it starts with training mistakes in puppyhood, as a sweet puppy is often allowed to get away with a lot. But when a dog grows up to be fully grown, pulling and tugging on the lead is suddenly no longer so easy and, depending on their size, an owner can struggle to handle them. Other reasons are impulses such as stress, fear, trauma or even boredom. Some dogs are very stressed when going for a walk and want to avoid meeting fellow dogs. Other dogs, for example, are very jumpy and thus pull in different directions. The good news is that lead-handling skills can be trained in every dog owner. However, when preparing, the focus must also be on the dog's behaviour when going out. Many dogs already run excitedly to the door and pull their owner out the door.

🐶 EXERCISE 41 🐶
Getting used to a harness (Indoor/Outdoor)

For lead training, a dog should ideally wear a well-fitting harness.

Step 1: Take your dog's harness and sit on the floor.

Step 2: Call your dog to you, rewarding him with a treat through the head opening of his harness.

Step 3: Repeat this exercise a few times and then wait until he's put his head through on his own. Reward him again.

Step 4: When you close the harness now, proceed gently, rewarding your dog with every step.

Exercise objective: Your dog enjoys putting on his harness.

🐶 EXERCISE 42 🐶
Going out of the house in an organised fashion (Indoor)

Your dog is already excited when he leaves the house. That's why you should first train him only to go out when he's calm.

Step 1: Put your dog on the lead, walk him to the front door and create distance between you both. Don't allow him to reach the door but encourage him to wait about one to two meters away with a loose lead.

Step 2: Command him to go "down" with the lead still loose. The commands "Stand" or "Stay" are suitable alternatives here. If he tries to push past you to the door, send them away and into the "Down" position. Do this exercise until it's possible to go out the door without any fuss.

Exercise objective: Your dog learns to understand that he's not the one to decide when he can go outside. In addition, walks become more relaxed because the stress is taken away beforehand.

🐶 EXERCISE 43 🐶
Exercise with the door
(Indoor)

Another variation is to teach your dog to go out of the house relaxed by learning that he has to coordinate it with you beforehand.

Step 1: Stand outside the front door with your dog on the lead.

Step 2: Open the door slightly. If he tries to push through past you, close it again.

Step 3: Open the door again and as soon he tries to squeeze through, close it again. Be careful not to hurt him.

Step 4: Repeat this exercise until he looks at you questioningly. When this happens, it's time to open the door and allow him to walk outside.

Exercise objective: Your dog makes contact with you before leaving the house and doesn't drag you out!

🐶 EXERCISE 44 🐶
Success without pulling
(Outdoor)

A good way to get a dog to stop pulling is by not associating it with a sense of achievement. The less success they feel about certain behaviour, the faster they'll refrain from it.

Step 1: Take your dog for a walk. As soon as he starts to pull, stay rooted to the spot and ignore him.

Step 2: As soon as he stops tugging, call him to you and reward him. Then, continue walking. Repeat this process until he's realised it's worthwhile not to pull.

Addition for advanced learners: You don't always have to reward your dog with treats. Suppose he shows the desired behaviour consistently and walks easily on the lead, you can reward him by praising or using environmental rewards, for example, by allowing him to sniff a specific spot as a special reward.

Exercise objective: Your dog learns that pulling isn't successful and will walk better on the lead in the future.

🐾 EXERCISE 45 🐾
Getting rid of the tug
(Outdoor)

For this exercise, your dog must be on a lead when walking.

Step 1: Throw a treat in the field or an exercise area out of reach so your dog notices and feels the urge to retrieve it.

Step 2: Stay calm, move and continue to hold the lead.

Step 3: Wait for him to stop pulling on the lead, and then call his name lovingly.

Step 4: Praise him if he makes direct eye contact with you and his lead remains slack.

Step 5: Now, you can move on, and allow him to retrieve the thrown treat.

Exercise objective: Your dog learns not to tug on the lead when a treat is up for grabs, but wait patiently until told to retrieve it.

EXERCISE 46
Small reward
(Outdoor)

This exercise rewards your dog whenever he walks on a loose lead. This exercise requires small treats.

Step 1: When you leave for your walk, put the treats in a small bag rather than in your jacket or trouser pocket, as this may cause your dog to fixate on them

Step 2: Begin walking, and whenever your dog walks loosely beside you, praise him with words like "Top", followed by a treat. Practise this over a more extended period.

Step 3: Keep delaying the praise word when he's walking well on a loose lead.

Exercise objective: Your dog associates the loose lead with something positive and recognises that this behaviour is rewarding for him.

6.4 Leash Handling

🐶 EXERCISE 47 🐶
Change of direction
(Outdoor)

This exercise is about responding to unwanted pulling by changing direction.

Step 1: Walk your dog and respond to each pull with a change of direction.

Step 2: Vary the exercise by changing the pace and direction.

Step 3: Make the exercise fun for him and announce each change of direction with encouraging words.

Exercise objective: Establish good lead-handling skills and keep your dog mentally active. Direction and speed change require a dog to think and concentrate fully.

Tip - Associate the lead with positive things:
At times, the problem for some dogs doesn't start with pulling on the lead but with a dislike of it altogether. If you have such a dog, it is advisable to completely reassociate the lead. If the old lead has caused many bad experiences, purchase a new one. Begin by linking the new lead with positive experiences. Put the lead on your dog during the meal- and playtime. Even during cuddle time, your dog should wear the lead from now on. As the lead has now been positively conditioned, your dog will no longer avoid it in the future but even look forward to being leashed.

Tip - Encourage them to walk on the lead:
Some dogs don't want to walk on a lead at all. In this case, please also take a look at the **tip "Associate the lead with positive things"** and build up a positive attitude towards the lead. Causes for dogs not wanting to walk on the lead can be that they're too hot

or cold, in pain or, as with puppies, they first have to process the stimuli. Exercise 53, "Dog freezes when he sees another dog", has proven to be very helpful for adult dogs.

🐶 EXERCISE 48 🐶
A dog is too distracted to move on (Outdoor)

Some dogs sniff blades of grass and become distracted while walking. Please note that there's no malice involved in this activity as dogs become so engrossed and part of their own world. For this reason, they would likely hear you if you called them.

Step 1: when your dog is "sniffing", calmly walk up to him and gently encourage him on.

Step 2: If he doesn't respond, put your hand around the end of the lead, i.e. where the lead is hooked, and pull gently. Please don't be rough here; a light tug will make most dogs responsive again.

Exercise objective: Your dog becomes responsive again through gentle touches and is encouraged to continue walking.

🐶 EXERCISE 49 🐶
Off-the-lead walking - preparation (Indoor/Outdoor)

It would be beneficial to teach your dog the basic rules of how to walk without a lead. For example, teaching him that taking off his lead doesn't mean he has to run off. Training preferably should start at home.

Step 1: Put the lead on your dog and command him to sit.

Step 2: When he's sitting calmly and relaxed, take off the lead.

Step 3: When you have unfastened the lead from his collar, give (to the still sitting dog) the command for free running (e.g. "Run" or "Go") and make a corresponding hand movement.

Addition for advanced learners: As soon as the behaviour is good indoors, increase the distraction as you progress.

Exercise objective: Your dog doesn't associate free running with the sound of the lead being released from his collar.

🐶 EXERCISE 50 🐶
Recalling the dog
(Indoor/Outdoor)

A reliable recall is one of the most important things a dog should master. In the best possible case, your dog should be recalled from any situation, making living together much easier as well as preventing many undesirable situations.

Step 1: Start training at home in low-distraction conditions.

Step 2: Think of a word you'll use only in recall training. Prepare treats.

Step 3: Begin by bringing your dog indoors and walking him around the house. Then turn to him and say your recall word, for example, "to me". If he reacts, reward him. Repeat this exercise a few times.

Step 4: Practise this process with your dog off the lead at home. Like before, say the recall word and reward him as soon as he turns and steps towards you. Repeat this a few times.

Step 5: Increase the difficulty, perhaps calling and rewarding him from another room.

Step 6: Continue training outside but with a lead on a tow line. In the beginning, call your dog ONLY when he's not distracted and be sure to reward him with a high-quality reward.

Exercise objective: Your dog learns to drop everything to run to you once you give the command for the recall.

Tip: Avoid calling your dog when you're almost certain he will not respond. Be sure to use opportunities when you know he's responsive. Using a drag lead is very useful at the beginning of the training. Furthermore, it's essential to pay attention to your body language. Don't make threatening gestures, such as leaning forward or staring into his eyes, when calling him. Also, never recall him using a stressed tone of voice.

🐶 EXERCISE 51 🐶
call the dog at heel with luring
(Indoor/Outdoor)

The command "Heel" is particularly helpful, for example, when crossing a street or in situations where you want your dog to stay close to you.

Step 1: Take a treat in your hand and lead your dog with the treat close to his nose.

Step 2: Reduce the distance from the treat to your dog's nose, increasing the time interval in which he receives the reward. For example, reward him only after every third step.

Step 3: Begin to remove the threat by only presenting your hand to him without a treat.

Exercise Objective: Your dog walks at heel.

With this variation, it can happen that your dog only concentrates on the treat. For dogs who have a short attention span, it may be difficult to get their attention but be patient.

🐶 EXERCISE 52 🐶
Heel walking with a rewarding word (Indoor/Outdoor)

For this exercise, you need small treats and a word to reward your dog, e.g. "Top".

Step 1: Start by commanding him to sit on your left-hand side.

Step 2: Begin walking in a left-hand circle and only when he walks beside you on foot, praise him with the reward word and treat.

Step 3: Once you have rewarded him, say "Heel" and continue walking. Repeat step 2.

Exercise Objective: Your dog walks at heel.

If he stops to sniff, it's not a big deal. Just call him over and continue with the exercise. Don't train for more than five to ten minutes a day, but do it more often. After several repetitions, the dog will have learned the heel command.

6.5 Encounter with other dogs

Dog encounters on a lead are often challenging for dogs because they're limited in their body language. Many dogs develop problems with other dogs of the same species, but these don't always arise from aggression. Some dogs get frustrated because they aren't allowed to go up to the other dog they want to play with. This kind of situation can make a dog develop symptoms of leash aggression. In addition, the dog population in urban areas is relatively high, and it's difficult for a dog to avoid other dogs. Because everything is obstructed, most human-dog teams approach each other head-on, which is exceptionally impolite in dog language. Typically, dogs prefer to approach in an arch, to try to make peace with the oncoming dog. However, this isn't possible and, therefore, often leads to exaggerated reactions on the lead or causes the dog to freeze, and refuse to walk any further.

Most of the time, dogs that have problems with encounters with other dogs develop leash aggression as a consequence of bad experiences. Maybe their owner didn't interpret their dog's body language correctly and forced them into contact despite not wanting any. Or perhaps, they were bitten or bullied by other dogs in the past.

Often the root of the problem is found in training mistakes, for example, if the owner doesn't offer alternatives and doesn't protect their dog when they need it the most. You need to be aware that a dog pulling on their lead is doing it for a reason, and scolding or even using force **doesn't** help but only intensifies the problem. Below **you'll** find exercises on how to manage issues with dog encounters.

🐶 EXERCISE 53 🐶
Passing other dogs
(Outdoor)

This exercise is suitable when an off-the-lead dog is approaching you both.

Step 1: Make sure that you don't have a pull on the lead but that the lead hangs loosely down. Don't hold your breath at the encounter, but breathe deeply.

Step 2: Follow your dog's movements with the lead and be careful not to tighten it.

Exercise objective: To take the tension out of a dog encounter.

In involuntary dog encounters, it's advisable not to make the situation more stressful for your dog by tightening the lead.

🐶 EXERCISE 54 🐶
Dog stiffens in front of other dogs
(Outdoor)

Your dog doesn't want to go any further and stiffens when he sees another dog from a distance. Your dog fixates on the other and wants to avoid the encounter, but the other dog is already too close. So, your dog resorts to using this stress management strategy.

Step 1: Avoid tightening the lead and do not try to pull your dog away.

Step 2: Then walk in front of your dog and direct him in the other direction using body language. Most dogs will then come out of their daze and react to their owner's movements.

Exercise objective: Your dog releases its stiffness and you can continue the walk.

Tip: Dogs usually show clear commands before the encounter they want to avoid. Pay attention to this next time and avoid them if necessary.

🐶 EXERCISE 55 🐶
Leading the dog on the averted side (Outdoor)

Some dogs don't want to have contact with other dogs, so it's often a good idea to walk your dog past the other dog on the opposite side of the pavement or road to spare him the stress.

Step 1: Position yourself between your dog and the opposing dog to form a buffer.

Step 2: When you're in position, walk casually past the other dog.

Exercise Objective: Act as a visual shield by walking between your dog and the other dog.

It increases their trust in you. In addition, the surprise effect ensures that your dog is distracted from the other dog.

🐶 EXERCISE 56 🐶
Threatening dog
(Outdoor)

Before dogs are put on the lead, they often start to fixate on each other. It's essential to recognise and stop this. This exercise is suitable for dogs that are still responsive in such a situation.

Step 1: You recognise that your dog is threatening another dog. He's fixated on the other dog; he slows his pace and straightens his route.

Step 2: Intervene by addressing your dog and command him to do something like sitting or another exercise that you know he enjoys or is good at.

Step 3: While keeping your dog busy, the other human-dog team can walk by.

Exercise objective: The dog's threatening behaviour is prevented in advance so that it doesn't lead to confrontation.

🐶 EXERCISE 57 🐶
Associating with other dogs in a positive manner
(outdoor)

For this exercise, you need a second human-dog team. Start the training from a great distance under controlled conditions. Furthermore, it would help if you had a praise word for the activity.

Step 1: Take your dog for a walk and spot another human-dog team from a distance.

Step 2: Your dog sees the other dog and remains calm. Say the word and reward your dog.

Step 3: If your dog doesn't react at a distance, slowly and gradually reduce the distance to the other dog. Your dog must have no reason to be put on the lead during training.

Exercise objective: Your dog associates other members of his species with something positive and will no longer show aggressive behaviour on the lead in the future.

Tip - Fear of other dogs:
Fear of other dogs can mean the dog doesn't want to get loose outside. If this is the case, it often helps to walk your dog in an area that isn't yet marked by negative experiences and has a smaller dog population.

6.6 My dog is afraid of...

Fear is deeply rooted in humans and dogs because it protects us from threats and makes us capable of reacting. While humans can talk about their anxiety, dogs express it through their body language and behaviour. A fearful dog often shows a crouched posture with their tail tucked in and ears flattened. Loud vocalisations such as whimpering and whining can also be observed in some situations. Similarly, symptoms such as trying to escape a fear-inducing stimulus and subtle commands such as heavy panting may be observed, even in cold temperatures. Licking their muzzle, looking around nervously, and refusing treats are also among the calming commands and can express fear. Dogs can fear many stimuli, the best known of which is probably fear of noises, such as thunderstorms or fireworks.

Furthermore, some dogs are afraid of other people and also children. It's essential to eliminate their fear because only then are they able to lead a stress-free dog life. If your dog is afraid, support him. The assumption that you shouldn't comfort your dog because otherwise, his fear will be intensified has been disproved. Of course, you shouldn't pity your dog beyond measure. But if he seeks your comfort and closeness when he's afraid, you should allow this.

🐶 EXERCISE 58 🐶
Fear of other dogs
(Outdoor)

This exercise is suitable for dogs that are afraid of other dogs. For this, you need another person with a dog and lots of high-quality treats. More about this can be found in chapter section 6.5.

Step 1: The other human-dog team positions themselves at a distance where your dog isn't yet showing fear commands.

Step 2: Whenever your dog looks calmly at the other dog, say your praise word and reward him with a high-quality treat that you know he loves.

Step 3: Repeat this exercise and gradually reduce the distance to the other dog. You must proceed slowly and give your dog time.

Exercise Objective: This desensitisation exercise is designed to get your dog used to seeing other dogs and, through reward, associate something pleasant with them.

6.6.1 Separation anxiety

Many dogs suffer from separation anxiety because they've never learned to stay alone in a relaxed manner. Dogs are pack animals and prefer to be with their caregivers all day. For this reason, it's necessary to teach your dog to stay alone gradually. It's best to start when they're a puppy, but adult dogs can also learn to be comfortable alone and without stress.

6.6 My dog is afraid of...

🐶 EXERCISE 59 🐶
Preparing to stay alone - disregarding the dog (Indoor)

Before leaving dogs alone for some time, measures must be taken. These preparations ensure that they learn from the beginning that they're not always the centre of attention and make it much easier for them to stay alone.

Step 1: You're at home and start reading a book or concentrating on something else.

Step 2: Your dog isn't getting any attention at all.

Step 3: Step by step, increase the amount of time your dog doesn't get attention from you.

Addition for advanced learners: If your dog has learned that he doesn't get constant attention just because you're at home means that you can vary the exercise by occasionally going into another room and occupying yourself elsewhere.

Exercise objective: Your dog learns that there are times when you're not available and this will later help him to be relaxed when left alone.

6.6 My dog is afraid of...

🐶 EXERCISE 60 🐶
Create a resting place
(Indoor)

A resting place is very helpful because dogs can retreat there again and again if something becomes too much for them.

Step 1: Prepare a place for your dog where he can relax. Maybe he's already chosen it, so you can emphasise this by making his chosen home cosy.

Step 2: Reward him calmly when you see that he's lying in his spot. For example, say "calm" or "relax".

Exercise objective: Your dog associates his place with absolute calmness and perceives it as a place of retreat whenever you leave home.

A feel-good place is essential when you start training your dog to stay alone.

🐶 EXERCISE 61 🐶
Leaving the flat
(Indoor)

Some dogs find it easier if you give them a command before you leave the house. This way, they know that you'll now be gone for some time and aren't constantly expecting your timely return.

Step 1: Before leaving home, give your dog a signal such as "Coming soon".

Step 2: Open the door and go outside.

Step 3: Repeat this twice a day, but at different times. Stay

6.6 My dog is afraid of...

away for a few seconds at a time, and slowly increase it to minutes.

Exercise objective: Your dog is used to you leaving home.

This exercise is especially effective if your dog isn't used to being left alone but doesn't show any signs of separation anxiety. It's essential that when you come home, you ignore him and don't overdo it when you greet him.

🐶 EXERCISE 62 🐶
Practice staying alone
(Indoor)

Practising staying alone starts at puppyhood but adult dogs some-times have to learn it too. Combine this training with the previous exercises 58 - 60.

Step 1: Ideally, use phases when your dog is busy, for exam-ple, sniffing or licking a food toy **cone**. Leave the room for a minute, then come back.

Step 2: Increase staying away minute by minute.

Step 3: Vary the times you leave him alone. Sometimes stay away for a minute, sometimes for five minutes. Ignore him when you come back. Increase the time you're away bit by bit, gradually and slowly.

Exercise objective: Your dog learns it's normal when you're not there.

🐶 EXERCISE 63 🐶
Conditioned relaxation as support with music (Indoor)

Conditioned relaxation is an excellent way to calm dogs and make them feel relaxed. This way, they're in the ideal mood to rest and sleep. This exercise can help relax dogs before they're about to be left alone. Studies have shown that soft classical music is best for this.

It would be best if you played soothing music for this exercise.

Step 1: You see that your dog is just relaxing in his preferred spot.

Step 2: Turn on soothing music.

Step 3: From now on, whenever you see that your dog is resting, turn on the music.

Exercise objective: Your dog associates the music with calmness and relaxes when the music is playing.

🐶 EXERCISE 64 🐶
Conditioned relaxation with Aroma oils (Indoor)

For this exercise, you'll need a scarf and a good quality aromatic oil such as lavender. Alternatively, you can drizzle some of the oil on a tea towel if you don't have a scarf handy.

Step 1: When you see that your dog is resting, put the scarf or tea towel around his neck or back. Never put more than one drop on the scarf or tea towel.

Step 2: If you notice that he cannot relax wearing the scarf, remove it again. Some dogs don't like the scent of aromatic oils, which should be respected.

Exercise objective: Your dog associates the scent of the aromatic oil with relaxation.

Suitable oils for relaxation are, for example:

Popular oils for stressed dogs include fennel, lemon balm, yarrow, lavender, orange, and rose. For stress, the following oils have proven effective: Geranium, Patchouli, Ylang-Ylang, Chamomile, Frankincense, Sandalwood, Orange Rosemary, and Bergamot.

Tip: Only use genuine essential oils without additives. You can recognise these by the Latin name on the label. First, check whether your dog likes the scent. Please use sparingly because dogs can smell much better than humans - one drop is usually enough.

Caution! Like many things, aromatic oils can cause side effects such as respiratory and skin irritation, intolerance, and more. Caution should be exercised, especially when using on puppies, pregnant bitches, dogs with epilepsy, weakened dogs, and dogs with high blood pressure. Even if you're treating your dog or yourself homeopathically, the following oils shouldn't be offered: Camphor, Peppermint, Thyme, and Chamomile. It's advisable to discuss the subject briefly with the vet beforehand to find out more about it.

🐾 EXERCISE 65 🐾
Utilisation before staying alone (Indoor)

Before leaving your dog alone, it's important to let him rest so he can relax. With this exercise, you can succeed.

Step 1: Before leaving your dog alone at home, take him for a walk so he can go to the toilet.

Step 2: When you're back after the walk, give him a food toy to help him settle down.

Plan enough time for this so he's not hyper when leaving the house.

Exercise objective: Your dog learns to stay alone without stressing.

6.6.2 Fear of Driving

Many dogs have problems with driving. The reason for this is usually insecurity or nausea.

🐾 EXERCISE 66 🐾
Getting used to the car (Outdoor)

It's necessary to accustom your dog gently to the car and to associate it instantly with something pleasant. This approach can help prevent your dog from developing an avoidance attitude towards the car.

Step 1: Stand next to the car with your dog. Play games with him or do exercises that you know he likes.

Step 2: Go so far as to feed him from their bowl next to the car or lay down a sniffing carpet for him to find treats.

Exercise objective: Your dog learns to relax next to or at the sight of the car and no longer shows avoidance behaviour near the vehicle.

🐶 EXERCISE 67 🐶
Getting used to opening the car (Outdoor)

Especially for young dogs, opening the car door can be strange. Therefore, it's essential to train in every single step.

Step 1: Proceed as in exercise 63. Pleasant distractions, such as licking a food toy, support this exercise.

Step 2: While he's relaxed, open the car door or sit in it occasionally.

Exercise objective: Your dog gets used to opening the car door and remains relaxed.

🐶 EXERCISE 68 🐶
Making the car a comfortable place to rest (Outdoor)

With the right exercises, you can even ensure that your dog enjoys riding in the car. It would help if you had lots of little treats and patience for the exercise.

Step 1: Walk your dog to the car.

Step 2: While your dog waits outside relaxed, distribute treats throughout the car. Of course, he should watch you doing this.

Step 3: Encourage him to look for the treats. In the best case, he goes into the car voluntarily, i.e. without a command.

Exercise objective: Your dog associates the interior of the car with positivity.

🐶 EXERCISE 69 🐶
Relaxing in the car
(Outdoor)

If your dog can relax in the car, it makes everyday life easier. Now begin with training him to stay in the car for a few minutes longer.

Step 1: If he now likes to get into the car, start by stocking the car with activities that take he can do longer than just eating treats. Perhaps put a chew bone or another food toy in the car.

Step 2: When he's relaxed in the car with his food toy or bone, start petting him.

Exercise objective: Your dog associates the car's interior with pleasure and relaxes as soon as he gets in.

🐶 EXERCISE 70 🐶
The car closes
(Outdoor)

If the previous exercises were completed successfully, start closing the car.

Step 1: While your dog is busy in the car with a chew bone or similar, close the door for a few seconds at first and see how he reacts.

Step 2: When he continues to chew in a relaxed manner, close the door and sit in the driver's seat.

Exercise objective: Your dog stays relaxed in the closed car for longer.

🐶 EXERCISE 71 🐶
Start the engine
(Outdoor)

Before you finally start moving with the car, get your dog used to the sound of the gate.

Step 1: Your dog lies relaxed in the car, and you sit in the driver's seat.

Step 2: Start the engine. Observe how he reacts. If he looks nervous, you may need to return to an exercise where he's not yet shown fearful behaviour.

Step 3: If he's able to remain calm and relaxed in this situation, praise and reward him with treats. Only switch on the engine briefly at the beginning and only as long as he remains calm and relaxed.

Exercise objective: Your dog shows no fear and remains relaxed when starting the engine starts.

🐶 EXERCISE 72 🐶
The car drives off
(Outdoor)

Now it's time to get down to the nitty-gritty because the car is driving off. If you've done everything right, this step should no longer be a problem.

Step 1: Sit in the driver's seat as your dog relaxes in the back seat or the boot.

Step 2: Start the engine and drive off, at first only going a few meters. Observe how he reacts. If he stays calm, everything is fine. If he responds anxiously, you may have to go back to **exercise 67** or **68**. If he seems relaxed, increase the distance you cover with the car more and more each day.

Exercise objective: Your dog can ride along relaxed for a few meters without fear.

This exercise is increased by walking around the block, one kilometre extra a day.

Tip: Depending on your dog's training level, you can tap into the particular exercise that fits best. When you have reached the point where you can already go further away with him, ideally link this with positive events, for example, going to the dog park or into the forest for a walk.

6.6 My dog is afraid of...

🐶 EXERCISE 73 🐶
Controlled exit from the car
(Outdoor)

Getting out of the car in a calm, controlled manner is very important. Avoid simply opening the door and letting your dog jump out at all costs. This way, accidents can happen, and you put yourself and other road users in danger.

Step 1: Go to the car's boot or back door, depending on where your dog is.

Step 2: Give him a "sit" command and slowly open the door. If he doesn't sit but tries to lunge forward, give him the "stop command" and try again.

Step 3: If he remains calm, open the door, put the lead on him and allow him to jump or lift him out.

Exercise objective: Your dog gets out of the car in a controlled manner and doesn't put himself or anyone else in danger by spontaneously jumping out.

🐶 EXERCISE 74 🐶
Dog barking in the car
(Outdoor)

If a dog barks in the car, it's a sign of stress and that they're not feeling good. It's advisable to integrate the exercises for relaxed driving. You'll need treats and chews.

Step 1: Let your dog get into the car and buckle him in.

Step 2: Take him for a short drive now and then, and stay in the car with him. If he remains calm, give him a high-quality reward or chew bone.

Exercise objective: Your dog perceives the car as a safe place over time.

If possible, drive to a place where people pass by from time to time. In the case where your dog bark at passersby from inside the car, keep rewarding him for moments when he's quiet. If he barks at something or someone from the car, ignore it. Never scold him because he'll think you approve of this behaviour and "bark along".

6.6.3 Fear of visitors/children/objects

🐶 EXERCISE 75 🐶
Taking away a dog's fear
(Indoor/Outdoor)

Desensitisation training is ideal for dogs afraid of certain things/people. They are gently accustomed to it. For this exercise, you'll need the help of another person.

Step 1: Stand with your dog at a distance from the other person so that he doesn't feel any fear.

Step 2: Praise and give him a treat whenever he looks at the person without showing fearful behaviour. Use a treat your dog loves, such as cheese or meat sausage.

Step 3: Day by day, gradually reduce the distance to the other person.

Step 4: The other person may then also throw treats. At first, a little further away and then gradually closer.

Exercise objective: Your dog learns that people aren't a danger.

Please don't overwork your dog and reduce the distance to the other person at a slow pace.

🐶 EXERCISE 76 🐶
Barking at the sound of the bell (Indoor)

If your dog barks whenever there are visitors, this can be very stressful for everyone. Therefore, you should desensitize him to other people. For this exercise, you need the help of another person.

Step 1: Instruct a second person to ring your doorbell. You tell her to ignore the dog completely.

Step 2: As soon as the doorbell rings and your dog barks, go with him to the door where you've placed a filled food ball.

Step 3: Toss the food ball to your dog and calmly greet your visitor while he's busy.

Step 4: The visitor sits on the sofa and takes the food ball away from your dog without comment.

Exercise objective: Your dog stays relaxed when you visit.

🐶 EXERCISE 77 🐶
Dog and person in one room
(Indoor/Outdoor)

Here, too, you need the help of another person.

Step 1: The other person must sit on a chair and completely ignore your dog (no talking to it, no looking at it, etc.).

Step 2: You are in the room with your dog who can move freely around.

Step 3: Any sign of interest by your dog to the stranger should be rewarded with praise and treats. If your dog gets too close, the person is free to increase their distance.

Exercise objective: Your dog can make contact with strangers in a safe setting and on his terms.

Tip: Never put a dog in a situation where they feel threatened by other people or children. Give them enough distance and desensitise them slowly (**exercise 75**). Never leave a dog unobserved with a stranger. In the worst case, fear-aggressive behaviour will react to the stranger's approach.

🐶 EXERCISE 78 🐶
Fear of the lift
(Indoor)

The fear of the hoover is widespread among dogs. For this reason, many breeders get the dog used to it when they're still a puppy. If this isn't the case, you could achieve success with this exercise:

Step 1: Enter a lift with your dog, rewarding him with a high-quality treat. Then leave the lift. Repeat this step three to four times.

Step 2: Go in again with your dog; this time, wait for the door to close, only then give him the treat and go out again. Repeat this step three to four times.

Step 3: As soon as you notice that your dog is getting calmer, increase the difficulty level by taking him to the next floor. You can use a toy as a distraction. Get off at another level and reward him.

Exercise objective: Your dog becomes calmer in the lift and loses his fear.

6.6.4 Fear of noise
Thunderstorms/fireworks/noisy vehicles etc.

It's assumed that dogs' intense fear of some noises is genetically determined. Furthermore, they probably never came into contact with such noise sources during their socialisation phase as puppies and are therefore insecure. Whether your dog is afraid of thunderstorms, fireworks or passing cars (such as trucks), counter-conditioning can be used to treat **all types of fear of sounds.**

🐾 EXERCISE 79 🐾
Fear of hoover
(Indoor)

Step 1: Place the switched-off hoover a few metres away from your dog so that the hoover is in his line of sight. Lure him towards the hoover with treats.

Step 2: Move the switched-off hoover calmly and slowly around. If he stays calm, reward him with a treat.

Step 3: Then, a second person takes over the hoover and turns it on in another room so it's still audible to your dog. You should stay, stroking and comforting him.

Step 4: The second person should slowly move towards your room door while you calm or distract your dog with a toy.

Step 5: If the hoover gets into the room and your dog remains calm, reward him with a treat. You must be patient and not overstress him as this could prolong the process.

Exercise objective: Your dog gets used to the hoover and the loud noises, and is able to remain calm during vacuuming time.

6.6 My dog is afraid of...

🐶 EXERCISE 80 🐶
Counteracting fear of New Year's Eve and thunderstorms
(Indoor)

For this, you need a CD with New Year's Eve sounds. These are now available in shops. You can also be sure to find them on YouTube. It makes sense to start the training a few weeks or months before New Year's Eve.

Step 1: Turn on the audio at a low volume.

Step 2: While the New Year's Eve audio is playing in the background, play with your dog or give him a chew bone. Do something special that he likes but doesn't get every day.

Step 3: Turn on the audio for a few minutes daily and spend time with your dog.

Exercise objective: Your dog associates the appearance of the fireworks with something pleasant.

🐶 EXERCISE 81 🐶
New Year's Eve measures
(Indoor)

In dog training, you should generally act with foresight, this way, you can save yourself a lot of stress. The stop command can also be useful here.

Step 1: On New Year's Eve, give your dog a good workout perhaps, taking him for a long walk or to do something exciting. In any case, attach him to the tow line but don't put on his lead.

Step 2: On New Year's Eve, **Give** him chewy snacks or a food toy. Anything they love is appropriate in this situation. Chewing and licking calms dogs immensely and reduces their stress.

Step 3: Close all blinds and curtains and turn on the music or the TV so the banging is drowned out.

Step 4: If your dog wants to retreat somewhere, allow this.

Exercise objective: Your dog gets through New Year's Eve as best as possible.

Tip: If your dog likes to retreat to a safe place during thunderstorms, a box is wonderfully suitable for this (see **exercise 29**). There are now even soundproof boxes on the market. Conditioned relaxation is also an excellent way to relieve your dog's stress if he's afraid of thunderstorms/New Year's Eve (see **exercises 69** and **70**).

6.7 Stopping your dog from Jumping at Someone

Many dogs start jumping or barking at their owners when they return home. Some dogs use barking/jumping as an **overreaction**. This is when a dog shows inappropriate behaviour because they're in an uncomfortable conflict situation. Most of the time, jumping during a walk is also because the owner isn't waking their dog on a loose lead but tightening it, increases their dog's excitement because they think something exciting will happen.

Jumping is a learned action and is often the result of training mistakes. Often jumping and barking have been unconsciously reinforced by the owner scolding the dog or trying to push it away. Both times the dog has received attention for its behaviour.

🐶 EXERCISE 82 🐶
Acting with foresight
(Indoor/Outdoor)

Step 1: You notice that your dog wants to jump up on another person.

Step 2: Give your dog a stop command (see section 6.1.4).

Step 3: When he looks at you, reward him.

Exercise Objective: By untying beforehand, your dog will focus his attention on you rather than on the other person.

🐶 EXERCISE 83 🐶
Greet people without your dog Jumping on them
(Indoor/Outdoor)

This exercise should be practised when your puppy moves in with you. Puppies can learn desired behaviour very early, which can lead them to not display inappropriate behaviour in later adulthood, including jumping up.

Step 1: Stand with your dog about five metres away from the other person.

Step 2: The other person says "hello" or another word of greeting.

Step 3: If your dog now keeps all four paws on the ground, praise and reward him.

Step 4: With each training session, reduce the distance to the other person.

Exercise objective: Your dog understands that it's worthwhile for him to keep on all fours instead of jumping up at other people.

🐶 EXERCISE 84 🐶
Don't let puppies jump at all
(Indoor/Outdoor)

Management methods are optimally suited for acutely stopping a behaviour. Nevertheless, they should be trained properly in the further course.

Step 1: Your puppy starts by jumping up at you.

Step 2: As soon as he does this, turn away and ignore him.

Step 3: Once he's on fours, reward him.

Exercise objective: Your puppy understands that he'll not get attention if he jumps on you and gets out of the habit.

This exercise is also suitable for adult dogs who like to jump when their owner comes home.

🐶 EXERCISE 85 🐶
Use treats precisely
(Indoor/Outdoor)

Step 1: Come home and prepared treats beforehand.

Step 2: When you come in at the front door, throw some treats on the floor away from you and let your dog look for them.

Exercise objective: Your dog doesn't reduce his energy surplus by jumping at the treats but by concentrating on finding them.

🐶 EXERCISE 86 🐶
The seat can – conditioning
(Indoor/Outdoor)

Even if your dog wants to jump up at you or other people in every situation, the seat box can do a good job.

Step 1: Fill a can with treats.

Step 2: Hold the can in front of your upper body and command your dog to sit.

Step 3: As soon as he sits, give him praise, open the can and reward him as a treat.

Step 4: After each session, take the can away again, and allow him to link it exclusively to the sit command.

Step 5: Repeat the exercise a few times until he understands that he shouldn't sit when he sees the can.

Exercise objective: Your dog sits down when he can see the can.

🐶 EXERCISE 87 🐶
The seat can prevent jumping people (indoor/outdoor)

Step 1: You get into a situation where your dog wants to jump on you.

Step 2: Have the seat box handy and show it to him.

Step 3: Give him a treat from the can when he sits down.

Exercise Objective: Your dog prefers to sit down instead of jumping up at you.

Increase the distractions gradually.

🐶 EXERCISE 88 🐶
Playing with the dog (Indoor/Outdoor)

Barking when the doorbell rings is often a sign of insecurity and fear. It's important to train this because it saves a dog a lot of stress. For this exercise, you need a second person and high-quality treats.

Step 1: Before entering your home, prepare the toy.

Step 2: As soon as you come in the door, throw the toy, for example, a ball, away from you. A stick could also work.

Step 3: At the beginning, stay close to the basket; if he gets up and barks, keep sending him back to his place.

Step 4: Repeat the steps and, if successful, gradually increase the distance and the reward period. In the beginning, imme- diately after the "go to place", then after 2 seconds, then after 4 seconds, etc., until you have reached the front door.

Exercise objective: Your dog no longer thinks about jumping you.

For dogs, playing is often more valuable than jumping, which is why this exercise is good for getting your dog out of the habit of jumping.

6.8 Understanding dog language: Barking, whining, whimpering

Barking, whining, whimpering, howling, and howling are all part of a dog's spoken language. There are dog breeds considered to be very fond of barking, such as herding dogs such as the Collie, the Bearded Collie, and the Sheltie. These dogs can get immersed in barking, so you must train them consistently and show them when it's time to stop. It's not always easy to interpret a dog's vocalisations correctly, as they're very versatile. Barking can express many emotions and sound aggressive, joyful, excited or even insecure. If you want to know the reason for your dog's barking, you need to interpret his body language while he's barking. If he barks with his ears back and his weight backwards, it may mean he's feeling insecure. If your dog barks with a low pitch of voice and it sounds somewhat threatening, he probably has heard something suspicious and wants to protect his territory.

On the one hand, whining can mean that your dog feels uncomfortable. Alternatively, he wants attention at the dinner table. Growling is to be understood as a warning and means that a dog wants distance and feels uncomfortable in a situation. *Never* forbid your dog to growl; otherwise, he may skip it and go straight to biting.

🐶 EXERCISE 89 🐶
Bark when it rings 2
(incl. visit)

An insecure dog can be distracted with the help of a food game. You need the help of another person here.

Step 1: Instruct the second person to ring your bell and ignore your dog for the entire exercise.

Step 2: As soon as the doorbell rings and your dog barks, go with him to the door where you've placed a filled food ball.

Step 3: Throw the food ball to him and greet your visitor while he's busy and distracted.

Step 4: Ask your visitor to sit on the sofa, and take the food ball from your dog without comment.

Exercise objective: Your dog remains relaxed when the doorbell rings and a visitor enters.

🐶 EXERCISE 90 🐶
Create an alternative behaviour to barking
(Indoor/Outdoor)

This exercise is about establishing an alternative behaviour. It can be any behaviour that your dog likes to do. A dog cannot do two things simultaneously, so they replace the barking with alternative behaviour. You'll need high-quality treats for this exercise.

Step 1: As soon as your dog starts barking, command him to "Sit".

Step 2: After showing him this alternative way to behave, give him high-quality rewards. Repeat this exercise consistently, and he will offer alternative behaviour rather than barking in certain situations.

Exercise objective: Your dog shows an alternative behaviour instead of barking.

🐶 EXERCISE 91 🐶
Dogs that bark because of hallway noises (Indoor)

If your dog barks at every noise in a block of flats, it can be very unpleasant. Try this exercise to avoid problems with the neighbours and unnecessary stress for your dog. This exercise is helpful if you live in a house with a high noise level and your dog barks at unfamiliar noises.

Step 1: Take your time and listen to the sounds in the hallway.

Step 2: Give your dog a treat whenever a sound is heard from outside.

Step 3: To prevent your dog from constantly expecting a treat, once the desired behaviour is established (i.e. he remains calm), begin to reward him on a rotating basis instead of every time. This way, you can refresh the behavior but the dog understands that he won't get a reward every single time.

Exercise objective: Your dog associates noises from the hallway with something pleasant and stops barking.

🐶 EXERCISE 92 🐶
Stopping the fence barking with the command "Stop"
(Indoor/Outdoor)

This exercise is designed for dogs that like to bark at the garden fence and find it difficult to stop. For this exercise, you need a well-established stop command. If you have not yet established this, go to **exercise 21** and train this command with your dog first.

Step 1: When your dog has learned the stop command well, say it as soon as he starts barking at the garden fence.

Step 2: Give him quality rewards and praise him only once he's stopped barking. Soon, he'll stop barking at the fence if you're consistent with the training.

Exercise Objective: Your dog will refrain from barking because he will be rewarded.

🐶 EXERCISE 93 🐶
Dog barking for attention
(Indoor/Outdoor)

This exercise is helpful if you have already established a praise word, i.e. a word you always say when your dog shows desired behaviour (**exercise 1**). In this exercise, you must consistently ignore your dog as soon as he barks as he will perceive any reaction to his behaviour as reinforcement.

Step 1: As soon as your dog starts barking at you, ignore him.

Step 2: Now wait for him to take a pause from barking and reward him in this break. If you have a praise word, say it during the bark break and give him the treat.

Exercise objective: Your dog associates "being quiet" with something positive and stops barking.

🐶 EXERCISE 94 🐶
Puppies whine / howl / squeal for attention (Indoor/Outdoor)

Sometimes puppies whine because they need to go to the toilet urgently. But they also often whine because this is how they show their owner that they want their attention. This exercise is suitable to prevent whining from becoming established as an attention command.

Step 1: If your puppy starts whining, wait for a break when he's calm and give him a task to keep him occupied.

Step 2: Start with light obedience training; teach "sit" or play with him.

Exercise objective: Your puppy won't even be tempted to whimper by doing small tasks and will give up on whimpering as a ritual. If learned as a puppy this will mean that he'll refrain from whimpering in adulthood.

🐶 EXERCISE 95 🐶
Adult dog whine/yelp/squeal for attention (indoor/outdoor)

Many dogs want to attract attention through their spoken language. Often this has been unconsciously reinforced by the owner. In this exercise, it's important to ignore your dog consistently.

Step 1: Ignore his whining.

Step 2: As soon as he shows calmness, reward him with attention. Be sure to pay attention to him when he's not whimpering.

Exercise Objective: Your dog stops whining to get attention.

Tip: If a dog starts whining out of the blue, there is always a reason so please go consult a vet. Dogs also, whine when they're in great pain.

6.9 Biting and snapping

There are many reasons why dogs bite. Most of the time, these dogs have not been socialised or have experienced trauma. Training errors are also reasons why dogs can bite. For example, a dog has learned that if they bite their owner's hand, their owner will ignore them. Most dogs show clear commands before they bite. If these are ignored, the bite will occur.

Training yourself in your dogs' body language is the first step toward bite prevention. Furthermore, a dog that bites should also wear a muzzle. Generally, every dog should receive appropriate muzzle training, preferably when they're still a puppy. The muzzle must be designed so they can pant and drink without problems.

Furthermore, it must not be too tight and allow free air circulation. It's advisable to get support from a trainer or veterinarian.

🐶 EXERCISE 96 🐶
Training puppy bite inhibition
(Indoor/Outdoor)

Puppies don't yet have bite inhibition when they come to their new home. It means they want to explore everything with their pointed baby teeth and don't shy away from human skin. The following exercise is excellent if your puppy likes to use its teeth in play.

Step 1: You're playing with your puppy, and suddenly he starts biting your hands.

Step 2: As soon as his teeth touch your skin, say "Ouch" or howl loudly in a loud and high-pitched voice, showing him that they've caused you pain.

Step 3: After making your pain known, turn away from him and consistently ignore him for a few minutes.

Step 4: When you feel he's calmed down, you can give him your attention again.

Exercise objective: Your puppy learns to bite inhibition and respectful interaction with people.

🐶 EXERCISE 97 🐶
Adult dog snaps
(Indoor/Outdoor)

This exercise is for dogs that have snapped out of the blue and have become accustomed to this behaviour.

Step 1: If your dog snaps at you, make a sound of pain to show him that what he did was wrong.

Step 2: Leave the situation, showing your dog that you don't want to harm him.

Step 3: If he walks away from the situation instead of snapping, give him a quality reward. Dogs always show calming commands before they snap. The better you recognise these, the better you can support your dog so that snapping doesn't occur.

Step 4: Take your dog to the vet for a check-up. Dogs usually don't bite for no reason; it could be that they're experiencing pain.

If the vet reassures you that your dog is healthy, find a trainer who works with positive reinforcement.

Exercise objective: Your dog gets out of the habit of snapping.

🐶 EXERCISE 98 🐶
Muzzle training
(Indoor/Outdoor)

Muzzle training is very important, especially when unforeseen things happen. You may have to take your dog on the underground or train, where muzzling is compulsory. It would help if you had a muzzle and lots of small treats for this exercise.

Step 1: Prepare the muzzle and place a treat inside.

Step 2: Call your dog to you, letting him eat the treat from the muzzle and praising him in the process. Repeat this until he accepts the muzzle perfectly.

Step 3: If he puts his head into the muzzle without problems, increase the time he stays in it.

Step 4: Now touch the back of his head with the strap of the muzzle as if you are closing it.

Step 5: When all steps have adequately worked, close the muzzle for only a few seconds at first. Then slowly increase the duration.

Step 6: If your dog accepts the muzzle, put it on him occasionally, for example, while you're doing the washing up.

Exercise objective: Your dog can wear the muzzle without feeling stressed.

Practise slowly. Use several weeks or months for this.

Note: Not all muzzles are species-appropriate. Please refer to the information on "the right muzzle" in chapter 6.9. Proceed slowly with the training. Use several weeks or months for this.

6.10 Hunting instinct

The hunting instinct is innate in most dogs and consists of the sequences of search and orientation behaviour - fixation - stalking - chasing - grabbing - killing - carrying away - eating. A herding dog can also have a hunting instinct, whereby the last sequence of hunting behaviour, i.e. killing the prey, has been bred out. A pronounced hunting instinct in a dog can be highly exhausting for the owner. It's almost impossible to let the dog run free because as soon as they've picked up a scent, they no longer listen and start to move toward the supposed prey. Furthermore, a pronounced hunting instinct can express itself in that the dog's nose only sticks to the ground when walking; they display nervous behaviour and want to go here and sometimes there, and so on. Other signs of a hunting instinct are that the dog freezes at the sighting of a wild animal and begins to lie down, wait for it, and perhaps even attempt to chase it.

You cannot train the hunting instinct out of a dog, but by building up impulse control through obedience exercises, they can learn to resist a stimulus. Furthermore, you can offer them a substitute activity for hunting, such as playing ball. Here, too, getting additional support from a trainer is advisable!

🐶 EXERCISE 99 🐶
Search for objects
(Outdoor)

A good way to give dogs an alternative activity to hunting is to let them search for objects. This gives them the best possible mental workout.

Step 1: Walk your dog in a quiet environment.

Step 2: Drop something inconspicuously during the walk, such as a pack of tissues.

Step 3: After a few metres, turn around and walk back. If your dog can find the pack and sniffs at it, praise and give him a treat.

Step 4: Subsequently, you can increase the difficulty by dropping the item in areas with more distractions, such as the forest.

Exercise objective: Your dog learns to use his nose in a concentrated way. It promotes mental exercise.

🐶 EXERCISE 100 🐶
Positive reinforcement – Avoiding Hunting avoidance of game and co.
(Outdoor)

Step 1: You notice that your dog starts to display hunting behaviour. For example, freezes when he sees an exciting stimulus.

Step 2: Praise and offer him an exciting activity that he likes, for example, a short game of tug-of-war, a treat hunt etc.

Exercise objective: Your dog learns that he's allowed to show the first sequences of hunting behaviour, for example, the search and orientation posture or fixation, but then, can be distracted with something pleasant.

🐶 EXERCISE 101 🐶
Laying a trail to replace hunting for game (Outdoor)

You'll need a good-smelling treat and a rope for this exercise. Your dog shouldn't watch you while you're laying out the trail.

Step 1: Knot the treat to the rope.

Step 2: Use the rope to drag the treat across the ground, for example, across the garden lawn.

Step 3: Now, hide the treat at the end.

Step 4: Bring your dog to the beginning of the trail and give the all-clear for tracking.

Exercise objective: Your dog is given a suitable alternative activity for his hunting instinct.

6.10 Hunting instinct

🐶 EXERCISE 102 🐶
Herding dog chases car/scooter/ bicycle (Outdoor)

Herding behaviour can be very stressful in everyday life. It's therefore essential to try and break your dog's habit. For this exercise, you need another person to drive with a particular object the dog is herding.

Step 1: Your helper drives the object at a distance from your dog. At this point, he shouldn't yet react to it.

Step 2: Reward him if he looks calmly at the object.

Step 3: Establish an alternative behaviour. For example, command your dog to "sit" when he sees the object. Reward him for this!

Step 4: Slowly and gradually reduce the distance to the object.

Exercise objective: Your dog gets used to moving objects and reacts calmly to them.

Tip: Chasing cars, scooter drivers, and the like is annoying and extremely dangerous. If your dog chases them, you should use impulse control exercises to train him.

🐶 EXERCISE 103 🐶
Dog chases squirrels and co.
(Outdoor)

Walking with a dog that likes to hunt is usually anything but relaxing. It can take a long time to break the habit, but it's worth it. For this exercise, you'll need a dragline, a toy and treats on your dog's harness.

Step 1: Prepare the treats and toy. Walk your dog on the lead.

Step 2: If your dog makes eye contact with a squirrel or other wild animals, call him to you in a high-pitched voice.

Step 3: Hold and give him the toy.

Step 4: When you see him running towards you, stop and play with the toy.

Exercise objective: You're more attractive and preferable to your dog than the squirrel.

Tip: Use targeted recall when necessary

6.11 Practical city training

Many dog owners live with their dogs in the city. The urban space places unique demands on dogs. Besides the millions of smells, a dog must learn to climb stairs, take the bus or train and accompany their owners to restaurants and shops. Some dogs even come along to their owners' workplaces. Due to structural conditions in the city, dogs have to learn not to walk toward other people or animals all the time but instead to wait obediently e.g. when the pedestrian lights are red.

Dogs that have previously lived in the country and then moved into a city flat can also suffer a kind of "culture shock", especially if they suddenly have to ride in a lift. The sensory overload in the city is easier for your dog to bear if you're his point of orientation. It's therefore essential to gently familiarise him with the city's unique features so that he becomes a calm companion in an urban environment. The following exercises will help you to do this.

🐶 EXERCISE 104 🐶
Lift ride
(Indoor/Outdoor)

Especially in the city, dogs must know how to use the lift. But it's also necessary if they have joint problems, for example, and can no longer climb stairs so well. Taking the lift is very exciting for some dogs, so it should be built up slowly.

Step 1: Prepare the treats and radiate calmness and composure.

Step 2: Enter the lift with your dog and command him to sit. Reward him when the lift starts moving, and he stays seated.

Step 3: Once the door opens, your dog should stay seated. Stand between the door so it remains open and then allow your dog to get up and walk out.

Exercise objective: Your dog learns to wait calmly during the duration of the lift and exits in a controlled manner. The risk of injury to him should be reduced to zero.

🐶 EXERCISE 105 🐶
Waiting at the traffic lights
(Outdoor)

As the traffic in the city can be very heavy, it's important that a dog doesn't simply run across the street but waits obediently until their owner permits them to cross. For this exercise, it would be very useful if your dog also knows the muzzle command.

Step 1: Walk your dog on a short lead to the traffic lights, stop and command him to sit.

Step 2: As soon as the traffic light turns green, ask your dog to stand up and walk orderly across the zebra crossing.

Exercise objective: Your dog doesn't pull and drag you across the zebra crossing. It can otherwise be hazardous.

🐶 EXERCISE 106 🐶
Waiting at the Platform
(Outdoor)

Even if you don't normally travel by train, life can change and so it's important to get your dog used to a train platform.

Step 1: Walk your dog to a train platform and reward any calm behaviour.

Step 2: When he's relaxed on the platform, lead him over to a place to sit, and reward him. Then command him to "sit" and reward again. Do little exercises that your dog likes so that he associates the platform with positivity.

Exercise objective: Your dog likes to stay on a train platform and feel as stress-free as possible.

🐶 EXERCISE 107 🐶
Waiting for the Bus and train (Outdoor)

Even if you usually travel by car, training your dog to ride the bus or train is worthwhile.

Step 1: When approaching the bus or train, keep your dog on a short leash close to you.

Step 2: Approach the entrance with your dog "on your heel" and reward him once you're inside.

Step 3: Find a suitable place which is ideally a bit out of the way, and let him sit between your legs so that he feels protected. If you've done the blanket training (exercise 32), take his blanket with you and let him lie on it for comfort.

Exercise objective: Your dog can ride relaxed on the train.

Don't forget the muzzle you have ideally already accustomed to (**exercise 98**).

Tip: Before taking your dog on a train ride, ensure he has burned off some energy beforehand and is well exercised. But it's important to not overwork him but slowly introduce the training. For example, only ride one station at the beginning and increase his duration on the train journey slowly.

🐾 EXERCISE 108 🐾
Resist odours
(Outdoor)

In the city, the risk of a dog finding edibles on the floor is much higher. You need high-quality treats that are better than what your dog "finds".

Step 1: Place an edible object, such as a bread roll, in a spot where your dog can't notice it. Then, put him on a lead and keep it short, preventing him from reaching the bread roll.

Step 2: Walk your dog past the roll and when he notices it, stop. Now, wait until he makes eye contact with you.

Step 3: If he makes eye contact, reward and praise him abundantly. Then lead him past the roll.

Exercise Objective: Your dog makes contact with you and doesn't simply pick up objects off the floor.

🐾 EXERCISE 109 🐾
Resist odours variation
(Outdoor)

To keep the exercise from becoming dull, you can mix them up.

Step 1: Repeat the process of exercise 108, but this time run past the object together with your dog.

Step 2: Use a tug toy and start "tugging" it. Alternatively, you can take another toy. The important thing is that he finds the toy more interesting than the object on the floor.

Exercise Objective: See Exercise 108.

🐶 EXERCISE 110 🐶
Walking up the stairs
(Indoor/Outdoor)

It would help if you had many threats for this next exercise.

Step 1: To start, find a staircase that isn't slippery. Then take the treats and walk beside your dog while sprinkling a treat on each step.

Step 2: Make sure he can see the steps clearly and that he walks on the broader side of the stairs. Additionally, reward him verbally and encourage him to retrieve the treats.

Exercise objective: Your dog learns to run upstairs without being afraid of them. It's essential that he sees the stairs well and isn't simply lured up them.

🐶 EXERCISE 111 🐶
Walking down the stairs
(Indoor/Outdoor)

Walking downstairs is more strenuous on a dog's joints than running up. So, it's important to ensure that your dog takes the stairs step by step rather than racing down.

Step 1: Walk down the stairs backwards so you can watch him at all times.

Step 2: Place treats on each step as your dog gradually walks down the stairs.

Step 3: When you get to the bottom, do a short game with him to release any tension.

Exercise objective: Your dog learns not to run down the stairs but to walk down in a calm and orderly manner. This minimizes the risk of injury.

🐶 EXERCISE 112 🐶
Relaxing in the park
(Outdoor)

If you live in the city, you'll definitely want to go for a walk in the park and relax on a park bench at some point. You need treats for this one. In this exercise, you'll learn how to relax your dog.

Step 1: Sit on a park bench and give your dog the "down" command. Position him so that no one accidentally steps on him.

Step 2: When he's lying still, reward him consistently. Pay attention to his body language and reassure him if he tenses up.

Step 3: Repeat the exercise several times by always spending a few minutes on a park bench when you go to the park.

Exercise objective: To take the stress out of the situation for your dog through training. In the park, a dog is exposed to many stimuli. They should get to know them without feeling pressured.

🐶 EXERCISE 113 🐶
Visiting a Restaurant
(Indoor/Outdoor)

Visiting restaurants can be very exciting but stressful for dogs. For this reason, they should be accustomed to them slowly.

Step 1: Before you take your dog to a restaurant, he should be encouraged to get loose and exercise.

Step 2: Find a place in the restaurant where your dog can relax and not be disturbed by other people, preferably under the table with you.

Step 3: Give him a down command and wait until he lies down. Then hand him a bone to occupy himself with. If you have already completed the blanket training (exercise 32) with your dog, take his blanket with you.

Exercise objective: Your dog can relax in the restaurant and not disturb anyone else.

🐶 EXERCISE 114 🐶
The perfect office dog
(Indoor/Outdoor)

Before you take your dog to the office, find a peaceful spot where he can feel at peace and where there's no traffic.

Step 1: Ensure beforehand that he's been able to go to the toilet and is sleepy.

Step 2: Give him the command to lie down in his place (ide-ally, you've done the cover training with him - exercise 32).

Step 3: Give him a food toy, like a chew bone to occupy himself with.

Exercise objective: Your dog stays stress-free in the office.

If you have already done the box training (**exercise 29**) with your dog, you can also put a box in the office and create a safe place for him.

EXERCISE 115
Mailbox
(Indoor)

This exercise is ideal when you aren't at home and your dog has the opportunity to respond to the postman. This is only applicable if you have a letterbox.

Step 1: Open and close the letterbox several times from the outside.

Step 2: As soon as your dog no longer responds, throw him treats through the letterbox. You can leave a note on the door asking your postman to participate in the exercise in the future.

Exercise objective: Your dog doesn't get restless as soon as the postman arrives.

6.12 Useful exercises for everyday life, personal hygiene and visits to the vet

Having a dog also means taking care of their body. Whether it's drying them with a towel, checking their eyes and ears or clipping their claws. There are situations that your dog has to endure, for which reasonable impulse control and high frustration tolerance are essential. Going to the vet is also associated with massive stress for many dogs. Exercises that prepare the dog for the examinations and promote cooperative behaviour are helpful here. It's best to get puppies used to this, but adult dogs can also learn collective behaviour.

🐶 EXERCISE 116 🐶
Set-up of the chin target
(Indoor/Outdoor)

The chin target is suitable for checking a dog's teeth or eyes through cooperation, for example.

Step 1: Hold a treat above your dog's head while presenting your palm. Your dog should place his chin on this.

Step 2: Guide the treat onto your palm so he follows.

Step 3: When your dog is lying with his chin on the palm of your hand. Praise him with a praise word and a treat.

Step 4: Repeat this exercise until he independently places his chin on your palm.

Step 5: Reward your dog if he keeps his chin on your palm. If he moves away, stop rewarding him.

Exercise objective: To develop your dog's cooperative behaviour and impulse control concerning allowing a (medical) examination.

🐶 EXERCISE 117 🐶
Examining the eyes via the chin target
(Indoor/Outdoor)

Step 1: Use the chin target command.

Step 2: When your dog has rested his chin on your palm, say "yes", for example, and look closely at his eyes. In between, keep rewarding him.

Step 3: When he takes his chin off your palm, stop looking into his eyes and rewarding him.

Exercise Objective: Your dog volunteers to have his eyes examined by you.

🐶 EXERCISE 118 🐶
Getting the dog used to examinations
(Indoor/Outdoor)

Start this training when your dog is relaxed and tired. You'll need a food tube or high-quality treats for this exercise.

Step 1: Encourage your dog to relax on a blanket and lick the food tube.

Step 2: While doing this, touch a part of his body, for example, his paws or ears.

Step 3: When he accepts this perfectly, start holding different everyday objects to him (e.g. claw scissors, a brush, etc.).

Exercise objective: Your dog gets used to examinations.

🐾 EXERCISE 119 🐾
Dry with a towel
(Indoor/Outdoor)

Although many dogs enjoy being dried off, some need to get used to it.

Step 1: Prepare a licking mat for your dog and coat it with something you know he likes.

Step 2: While your dog is occupied with the licking mat, start gently stroking his body with a towel.

Step 3: Start drying his paws, followed by his whole body.

Exercise objective: Your dog accepts drying and doesn't develop avoidance behaviour towards it.

🐾 EXERCISE 120 🐾
Being lifted onto the table
(Indoor)

This exercise is ideally done with a puppy. You need a table and a non-slip blanket.

Step 1: Gently pick your puppy or dog up and give him treats.

Step 2: Be sure to have a non-slip blanket positioned on the table and place him on it. Then reward him abundantly. Hold him securely by the harness with one hand and feed him with the other.

Exercise objective: Your dog likes to be lifted onto the table to be examined.

🐶 EXERCISE 121 🐶
Getting used to the vet
(Outdoor)

Find a vet near you and ask if you can come for a training visit.

Step 1: Enter the vets and reward your dog as soon as you arrive.

Step 2: Let him explore and make contact with the vet and receptionist.

Step 3: Explore the veterinary room together, letting him get familiar with the different scents. Reward him extensively and then leave.

Exercise objective: Your dog learns about the vets under low-stress conditions and associates it positively.

🐶 EXERCISE 122 🐶
Calm lateral position
(Indoor/Outdoor)

Step 1: Command your dog to lie down and reward him.

Step 2: Then position a treat so that he lies on his side. If he lies on his side, reward him profusely.

Step 3: Then gradually increase the time he has to lie on his side. Initially, reward him for a few seconds and then for more.

Step 4: When he's become accustomed to lying on his side, gently examine his body, for example, starting at the paws and working upwards to the head.

Exercise objective: Your dog can be examined in the lateral position without stress.

🐶 EXERCISE 123 🐶
Bathing the dog
(Indoor)

An important exercise is bathing your dog properly. For this, equip your shower or bathtub with a non-slip pad.

Step 1: Gently accustom your dog to the bathtub, familiarising him with all the utensils. Be sure to reward every effort in the bathroom.

Step 2: Lift him into the shower or bath and reward him.

Step 3: First, turn the water up slightly and check how he reacts. Make sure that the water temperature is correct. It should be pleasantly warm rather than too hot or too cold.

Step 4: Start by lathering the dog from the legs upward. The head comes last, and it's preferable to wash it with a wash-cloth. Reward the dog after each step.

Exercise objective: Your dog associates bathing positively.

In addition to impulse control exercises, providing your dog with appropriate training should be part of everyday life. In the following chapter, you'll learn how to offer your dog activities that give him pleasure and, at the same time, promote his impulse control and frustration tolerance.

Note: Only bathe your dog "as often as necessary and as little as possible". Bathing too often dries out a dog's skin and can lead to irritation, among other things. Not bathing at all promotes unpleasant odours, unwanted bacteria, and yeast fungi. At the same time, it can often be a form of therapy for allergic dogs. Ideally, you should discuss this subject with your vet and find out what is the most suitable shampoo for your dog.

🐶 EXERCISE 124 🐶
Indoor sports with the dog, squats (Indoor)

Do you like to do sports at home, and your dog looks eager to join you? Then let them participate.

Step 1: Stand hip-width apart and lower your hips, keeping your weight on your heels and straightening your chest. When you look down, your knees shouldn't go beyond your toes.

Step 2: Your dog should stand in front of you or to your side and look at you. To engage your dog in this activity, give him a down command when you squat and an up command when you come back up.

Step 3: Step 3: Repeat the exercise. Support the instructions with treats and hand commands. Start slowly and increase the speed gradually.

Exercise objective: You can exercise at home in peace along with your dog. In addition to impulse control exercises, it should be part of everyday life to exercise your dog properly. In the next chapter, you'll find 21 practical mental exercises that are ideally suited for your dog's mental and physical exercise. In this way, you can offer your dog activities that give him pleasure and, at the same time, promote his impulse control and frustration tolerance.

– CHAPTER 7 –

Bonus Exercises:
Brain Games for Dogs

Brain games for dogs are suitable for strengthening impulse control and frustration tolerance. Furthermore, the human-dog bond is supported, the ability to concentrate is enhanced, and anxiety and stress are alleviated. In this chapter, you'll find exercises for outdoor and indoor use that are very suitable for exercising and encouraging your dog indoors in bad weather.

🐶 BONUS EXERCISE 1 🐶
Classic treat throwing game
(Indoor/Outdoor)

Dogs love treats, but they also love to romp and play. This game optimally satisfies both needs.

Step 1: Prepare lots of small treats and throw them away from you in your dog's direction.

Step 2: Command him to sit or go down.

Step 3: Throw the treats away from you and give him the go-ahead to search.

Step 4: Vary the exercise by having your dog look for the treats on the ground one time and catch them up in the air another time.

This simple exercise is fun for the dogs because they must concentrate and satisfy their hunting instinct.

🐶 BONUS EXERCISE 2 🐶
Toilet roll game 1
(Indoor)

Toilet paper rolls are a good and inexpensive way to create a challenging game for your dog.

Step 1: Take a few toilet paper rolls and fill them with treats. Fold the rolls in at the end so that they're sealed.

Step 2: Give your dog the sit command, placing the rolls in front of him.

Step 3: Give him the all-clear and watch the joy that he gets from shredding the rolls.

This exercise also trains impulse control because a dog must wait for the release. Furthermore, dogs love to bite objects. In this exercise, your dog releases energy and gets his needs fulfilled.

🐶 BONUS EXERCISE 3 🐶
Toilet roll game 2
(Indoor)

This exercise is a little more elaborate. You need toilet paper rolls, a cardboard box and lots of treats.

Step 1: Place the toilet paper rolls upright in the cardboard box tightly close together so that they fall directly when you poke them.

Step 2: Place the treats into the toilet paper rolls.

Step 3: Give your dog the all-clear to search for the treats in the box.

This exercise is a little more complicated but requires your dog to use his brain more. Working for his treats promotes your dog's self-confidence and frustration tolerance.

🐶 BONUS EXERCISE 4 🐶
The classic sniffing rug
(Indoor)

You'll need a sniffing rug or a towel.

Step 1: Hide many small treats or your dog's food ration in the sniffing rug/towel.

Step 2: Command him to wait in the sit or down position until you give the go-ahead to search.

A sniffing carpet offers all kinds of advantages. It promotes concentration and keeps your dog busy and tired. It's lovely for rainy days.

🐶 BONUS EXERCISE 5 🐶
Hiding treats indoors
(Indoor)

A game that is especially valuable on rainy days is hiding treats around the house. This allows the dog's nose to really get some exercise.

Step 1: Give your dog the down command.

Step 2: Hide treats all over your home.

Step 3: Give him the all-clear to search and help him find the treats.

This exercise is good for strengthening impulse control and intensifying the bond between humans and dogs.

🐶 BONUS EXERCISE 6 🐶
The towel cinnamon bun
(Indoor)

Every dog owner has a towel at home; the good news is that you can also use it to keep your dog busy. So, it would help if you had an old towel and lots of little treats.

Step 1: Lay the towel on the floor and put the treats on it. Then roll up the towel to make it look like a cinnamon bun

Step 2: Command your dog to sit and place the rolled towel in front of him.

Step 3: Signal the release and watch how he solves the task.

Many dogs love figuring out how to unroll the towel. This exercise is enjoyable for both dogs and humans.

🐶 BONUS EXERCISE 7 🐶
Hide and Seek at home
(Indoor)

Searching for objects is mentally exhausting for dogs and is fun for them. For this exercise, you'll need one of your dog's toys.

Step 1: Give your dog the down command.

Step 2: While he's waiting patiently, hide his toy around the home.

Step 3: Once you've hidden it, return it to him and give him the all-clear to search.

This exercise strengthens impulse control and the human-dog bond.

🐶 BONUS EXERCISE 8 🐶
Newspaper balls
(Indoor)

All you need for this exercise is newspaper and treats.

Step 1: Spread out the newspaper and scatter treats on it. Then wrap it up in more layers of newspaper to form a ball. In between each layer, place a few treats.

Step 2: Command your dog to sit.

Step 3: Throw the paper ball and signal the release.

This exercise is straightforward, and most dogs like it. However, if your dog likes to eat newspapers, refrain from this exercise.

🐶 BONUS EXERCISE 9 🐶
Treat search in toys paradise
(Indoor)

This game is a paradise for dogs. You'll need a plastic tub and plenty of your dog's favourite toys and treats.

Step 1: Put your dog's toys, for example, cuddly toys, balls, etc., in the tub.

Step 2: Throw treats into the tub.

Step 3: Let him search for the treats.

This exercise is suitable indoors and sweetens a rainy day for you and your dog.

🐶 BONUS EXERCISE 10 🐶
The Little Hats game
(Indoor)

This exercise encourages your dog to use his head properly. You'll need three plastic or yoghurt cups and treats.

Step 1: Command your dog to lie down.

Step 2: Once he's lying down, place the cups in front of him and put treats under one of them. Then move the cup around and give him the go-ahead to search.

Step 3: He should uncover each treat with his paw or nose.

This exercise is perfect for strengthening frustration tolerance and impulse control.

🐶 BONUS EXERCISE 11 🐶
Ambushing and hunting prey
(Indoor/Outdoor)

This game is really fun for dogs with an affinity for hunting. You'll need sticks for this exercise or one of your dog's toys.

Step 1: Command your dog to sit.

Step 2: Wave the stick or toy around in front of him.

Step 3: Give him the OK, and allow him to chase after the toy. Make sure to vary the exercise. Perhaps, wave the toy around on the ground, then in a figure of eight through your legs.

The exercise strengthens impulse control and the bond between humans and dogs.

🐶 BONUS EXERCISE 12 🐶
The tree track
(Outdoor)

This exercise combines mental exercise and is also nice for you to be out in the fresh air. It would help if you had good-smelling treats ready for a walk in the forest.

Step 1: Give your dog the command to sit.

Step 2: Take a treat and rub a trail along a tree.

Step 3: Afterwards, put the treat into the tree bark and give your dog the release.

The exercise is suitable for exciting walks in the forest and promotes impulse control.

🐶 BONUS EXERCISE 13 🐶
Hide and Seek in the forest
(Outdoor)

Dogs love searching for objects in the forest because they get to know completely new smells and have to concentrate. For this, you need a food dummy.

Step 1: Command your dog to lie down.

Step 2: Then go into the forest and drop the dummy any-where.

Step 3: Give your dog the release, and allow him to search for it. When he's found it and brought it back to you, reward him with a treat from the food dummy.

This exercise is perfect for keeping your dog mentally occupied, as he must use his nose intensively during the search.

🐶 BONUS EXERCISE 14 🐶
The sniffing course
(Indoor)

For this exercise, you'll need different things to hide treats in, for example, a sniffing carpet, a towel, newspaper and toilet paper rolls.

Step 1: Send your dog to another room while setting up the sniffing course.

Step 2: Fill the toilet paper rolls as shown in **bonus exercise 3,** make the towel swirl as shown in **bonus exercise 6** and make a newspaper ball as shown in **bonus exercise 8.** When you have finished, place the items one by one.

Step 3: Call your dog, command him to sit and then give him the go-ahead to sniff his way through the course.

This exercise is ideally suited as an indoor activity.

🐶 BONUS EXERCISE 15 🐶
Trick training "Turn yourself"
(Indoor/outdoor)

Dogs who like to learn new things will love this exercise. You'll need treats and a motivated dog.

Step 1: Hold the treat in front of your dog's nose and lead him around in a circle with it.

Step 2: Give him the treat as soon as he's back in the starting position.

Step 3: When he's circled a few times, sneakily remove your hand movement from the exercise by holding your hand higher and higher. Furthermore, before your dog makes the turn always say the command "Turn".

Your dog will quickly perform the turn-on command with a bit of practice. don't forget to reward him.

🐶 BONUS EXERCISE 16 🐶
Slalom through the legs
(Indoor/Outdoor)

Weaving through the legs is fun for a dog and trains their coordination.

Step 1: Get your dog to sit next to you. Then begin to take action by luring him with treats. Repeat this with each leg and draw your dog through each leg, again and again.

Step 2: When he's learned to go through your legs, start to introduce the command. Each time you send the dog through your legs say "through", for example.

With a bit of practice, he'll soon master the art of weaving through your legs. The exercise is perfect for strengthening a dog's concentration.

🐶 BONUS EXERCISE 17 🐶
Play hide and seek together
(Indoor/Outdoor)

This exercise will make you feel nostalgic. Try the game of your childhood with your dog; he'll will love it.

Step 1: Command your dog to sit and go and hide in the house or garden.

Step 2: Call out to him for release and allow him to try and find you. When he's found you, reward him with lots of petting or treats.

This exercise trains impulse control and strengthens a dog's self-confidence. Furthermore, it's very suitable for training and consolidating recall.

🐶 BONUS EXERCISE 18 🐶
Search game with grid ball
(Indoor/Outdoor)

For this exercise, you need treats, a cage ball, and filling material, for example, newspaper. If your dog tends to eat newspaper, use fleece strips instead.

Step 1: Fill the cage ball with treats and the newspaper.

Step 2: Command your dog to sit, place the ball on the ground and give him the go-ahead.

This exercise can be varied as you don't only have to give the ball to him but you can also hide or throw it.

🐶 BONUS EXERCISE 19 🐶
Treat diving
(Indoor/Outdoor)

Dogs that like water benefit from this game. For this exercise, you need a shallow bowl, water and treats.

Step 1: Command your dog to sit.

Step 2: Fill the bowl with water and throw in treats.

Step 3: Place the bowl in front of your dog and give him the go-ahead to dive in for treats.

This exercise is particularly suitable for hot days to encourage extra water intake.

🐶 BONUS EXERCISE 20 🐶
Which hand?
(Indoor/Outdoor)

It's an exercise that trains your dog's brain and keeps him busy. You'll need treats for this one.

Step 1: Command your dog to sit and kneel.

Step 2: Show him the treat in your hand and then close both hands into a fist. Now, it's time for him to guess which hand the toy is in.

Step 3: Give him the treat if he's able to sniff the correct hand. If not, let him try again until he's able.

This exercise strengthens your dog's frustration tolerance.

🐶 BONUS EXERCISE 21 🐶
Give your dog a Massage
(Indoor)

Who doesn't like being massaged? Your dog will love it too.

Step 1: Start the exercise when your dog is already relaxed and exercised.

Step 2: Sit with him on the sofa or even on the floor and talk gently to him. Start massaging him while paying attention to his body language and respect his appeasement commands.

This exercise is perfect for relaxing your dog and strengthening the dog-human bond, which will also affect your dog's behaviour outside.

– CHAPTER 8 –

Exercising Plan for your dog's first year

T he puppy period is one of the most beautiful times in a
person's life. Here the foundations are laid for the rest of
your life; you get to know your dog and begin to train
him to become a confident dog. In the following chapter, you'll find
a guide for your first year with your dog. The development of a dog
and the different phases of development are discussed.

Furthermore, you'll find tips and tricks on promoting your pelt-
nose's impulse **control** and frustration tolerance.

Basis of impulse control and frustration tolerance
In the first **weeks 1 - 3**, the basis for frustration tolerance and stress
resistance is laid. Examples of impulse control in the first three
weeks would be that every puppy has to wait until they can suck on
their mother's teat or also that they've to be patient until their
mother licks them. Playing with their siblings teaches the puppy so
much about impulse control and frustration tolerance. Furthermore, the breeder's behaviour plays a significant role by
distinguishing whether the puppy desires attention with its behaviour or whether an absolute need for satisfaction is the motive.

Establishing a secure and safe setting is essential in weeks 3 - 5 of
the puppies' life. In this phase, it's straightforward for puppies to
associate certain (security) stimuli with relaxation, as they cannot
yet feel any fear. They feel a sense of security when they come into
contact with these stimuli again later. During this time, puppies are
curious, full of joy and want to explore the world. As a responsible
breeder, you should take advantage of this. If you don't surround a
puppy with different stimuli in this phase, they may develop deficits in some areas, which they can no longer correct. It can lead to
behavioural problems later on.

An example would be if a puppy is cared for exclusively by one person and grows up in a puppy room. In this setting, there are too few stimuli with which they can associate the feeling of security. Even though they may have been treated well, they'll not be able to retrieve any or only a few security stimuli in their brain, which automatically leads to difficulties.

From **weeks 8 - 12**, the so-called **socialisation phase**, a puppy arrives at their new home. Here the new family must know the difference between encouragement and excessive demands. The more security stimuli the dog has gathered in its upbringing, the better the transition into a new living situation will be. It's now of great importance to socialise the puppy accordingly. It's not enough if they only get to know the garden and the house. It's essential to ensure that they're moderately encouraged. This includes controlled contact with fellow dogs, social contact with people and getting to know different environments. Over-exertion should be avoided at all costs, and long walks and hikes should also be a no-go at this age. For a long time, the rule of thumb, when it came to walking was five minutes per month of a puppy's life. However, this rule is now outdated. But make sure you don't overexert your puppy and give them enough time to sleep and rest.

Early warning signs that a puppy lacks impulse control are that it cannot settle down, run nervously, and whimpers all the time. This behaviour isn't normal because to lead a happy life, dogs need enough sleep; a puppy even up to *22 hours a day*. It's essential to distinguish whether a puppy only has five minutes of "puppy madness" and then quietens down or whether the behaviour is consistent and doesn't subside. In this case, it's essential to take educational measures because the behaviour will not reduce. Otherwise, you'll have a dog that is permanently hyperactive, hyper and nervous.

A dog's **first fear phase** also occurs between **weeks 8 and 12.** As a result, you have to be extremely sensitive, especially when socialising with your dog at this stage.

Tip: When buying your puppy, you should get an accurate picture of the kennel and the mother. it'll indicate how the puppy will most likely develop.

The first weeks at home
Usually, a puppy moves into its new home between **weeks 8 - 12 of life.** Use the first week to get your dog used to the new living environment. Confrontation with too many new stimuli should be avoided. However, it's crucial that you already start with housetraining (chapter section 6.2). It would help if you started with socialisation when he's settled in his new home. He must get to know people and other dogs without stress. In addition, he should already be accustomed to driving and - especially if you live in the city - to certain everyday stimuli. Public transport, restaurant visits and different surfaces (asphalt, meadows, gravel paths) are just as much a part of this as a visit to the workplace (chapter section 6.11).

To get used to other dogs and build up good social behaviour, it's advisable to visit a well-controlled puppy group (as soon as your dog has been vaccinated), where they can have positive experiences. However, don't overwork your dog because the acclimatisation to new stimuli should be highly measured. One aspect that is usually forgotten in the socialisation of puppies is that they should get used to being touched. You should therefore introduce your puppy to any examinations from an early age. It can take the stress out of going to the vet later on. Carry out the exercises in Chapter 6 regularly.

In summary, a dog should learn the following things in its social-isation phase:

- House-training
- Social contact with people and fellow dogs and other animals (e.g. horses)
- Getting used to moving objects (joggers, scooter drivers, cars, trucks etc.)
- Getting used to sounds and different surfaces
- Getting used to physical contact from caregivers as well as strangers
- Sufficient rest (22 hours per day)
- Cautiously getting to know children - ensure a puppy can withdraw anytime!
- Getting used to the lead, harness and collar
- Practise walking on the lead for short walks

Valuable exercises for the puppy

- House-training exercises
- Creat training
- Rest exercises
- **B**asic obedience exercises
- Incorporating thinking games into everyday life
- Small impulse control exercises such as encouraging eye contact

The puppy period ends with the beginning of the change of teeth. From about the **18th week of life,** your puppy is a young dog. During the evolution of teeth, dogs tend to chew on everything. It's best to put everything sacred to you out of his reach. Offer him toys, chewing bones and food toys he can chew on.

When dogs are young, new synapses are formed in their brain and networks are created through targeted cooperation with the owner. It would help if you used this time to build up an intensive relationship with your dog and teach him the behaviour you expect from him in the future. In this phase, consistent and loving training of your dog is essential.

Within the **4th and 10th months,** the dog's **second fear phase takes** place, which lasts about three weeks on average. In this phase, your dog might react more anxiously to unknown and already-known stimuli. Once again, you must not overwork him but support him when he reacts more sensitively because situations that frighten a dog during this time become very stubbornly ingrained. The solution is to make such cases pleasant for your dog by slowly getting him used to the fear-inducing stimulus with treats, praise and a confident demeanour.

Things you should encourage in your young dog:

- Consistent, loving training
- Exercises for impulse control
- Extending basic obedience
- Establishing and strengthening lead leadership

Adolescence 5th to 24th month of life, including puberty
Youth is generally reached when **sexual maturity** occurs. Of course, this cannot be generalised as the maturation of a dog depends on the breed and character. Depending on the breed, adolescence can **last until the second year of life.**

7. to 12. month of life
Puberty begins approximately when the bitch comes into heat for

the first time, and the male dog begins to lift his leg. The sex hormones become active at this time, and the dog enters the flailing years. It can mean that they may seem to have forgotten things they've already learned. Many dog owners don't recognise their dogs during this time. Similar to teenagers, the young dog's brain is also one big construction site at this time.

The first signs that your dog is approaching **puberty** are that he explores his environment more independently and sniff outside for longer and more intensively. In general, it can be said that dogs entering puberty have a higher stress level. Many dogs start to establish self-rewarding behaviour, such as barking, jumping and chasing. Marking behaviour also becomes more intense, and many males and females begin to scratch after marking. Behavioural problems such as following moving objects (cyclists, cars, scooters etc.) are also common. Another indication that your dog is now in puberty is that he shows more mouth activity. It means that he's got an even greater need to chew on things.

Furthermore, he may now try to claim specific resources for himself. If he was previously indifferent to a strange dog approaching his toy or chewing bone, he might now begin to overreact. Also, at this time a dog is no longer stress-resistant and has a thinner nervous system. Nevertheless, you should be consistent and offer him rules and rituals.

Valuable exercises for **puberty** are:

- Incorporating rest exercises and relaxation into everyday life
- **Introducing a**lternative occupation possibilities with an increased hunting instinct.
- Giving a dog plenty to chew and lick as this calms and de-stresses them.

- Integrating impulse control exercises into everyday life to a greater extent.

- Brainteasers in which they can use their nose

- Providing rituals and structure

- Mental workload through brain teasers

- Consistently carrying out obedience training and impulse-controlled training.

Maturation phase 12 to 18 months of life
During this phase, your dog matures into an adult quadruped. Some breeds grow faster than others. At this stage, a dog's basic framework is already in place, and its character and heritage traits are now showing. If you have consistently trained your dog up to this stage and built a solid foundation of trust, you'll now be able to reap the rewards. Of course, dogs are lifelong learners, but depending on the experiences your dog has had in the last few months, it'll show how mentally stable he is. Make sure you treat him right and treat him well.

CLOSING WORDS

As described in detail in the previous chapters, establishing a high level of impulse control and frustration tolerance is essential in dog training. This guidebook aims to help you lead a *stress-free* and *calm* life with your dog. From the exercises for impulse-controlled training to the bonus chapter with various activities for your dog, the content is well thought out and easy to put into practice in your day-to-day lives. After all, there's more than one way to achieve your goal.

You'll experience many ups and downs in your life together with your dog. However, you must use appropriate training methods and allow him to explore his environment confidently. This includes understanding his body language and establishing a predictable daily routine. Rituals and structures in the dog-human daily routine strengthen the bond and enable stress-free togetherness when life gets hectic. Especially when your dog enters puberty, you may sometimes not recognise him.

It's essential to remain consistent and not lose your sense of humour. Learning self-control and becoming tolerant of frustration is part of a dog's life. The more you practise the exercises with your dog, the more incredible both of your life together will become. Grow together, and you will recognise yourself in your dog and vice versa. Don't forget that your dog doesn't mean any harm if he disobeys you, and don't scold him. He simply doesn't know any better at that moment. It is your job to make him understand what you want from him. Many dog owners ask too much from their dogs too quickly and get frustrated when the exercises don't work right away. However, no master has ever fallen from the sky, so you should gradually increase the difficulty level in training. If you take this to heart, you will be able to recognise and appreciate the small successes much more quickly and efficiently.

The findings of this guide are based on the current state of science and service to support you in the best possible way in dog training.

For severe aggression or other behavioural problems, please seek help from a veterinarian or a dog trainer.

Last but not least:

Have fun training and growing together into a strong

human-dog team!

Many thanks

We hope you enjoyed the book. If you have any questions, sugges-tions or feedback, please feel free to send an email to Info@siimpo.de.

We would also be pleased to receive a review on Amazon. To leave a review please scan the following QR-Code or follow the Link https://amzn.to/41LPFL9.

EXERCISE DIRECTORY

6.1 BASIC EXERCISES FOR SELF-CONTROL & OBEDIENCE

EXERCISE 1	"WELL DONE" – COMMAND CONDITIONING 40	
EXERCISE 2	SET UP THE COMMAND "SIT" 41	
EXERCISE 3	CAPTURE THE COMMAND "SIT" 42	
EXERCISE 4	SET UP THE COMMAND "DOWN" BY LURING 43	
EXERCISE 5	SET UP THE COMMAND "DOWN" BY LURING 2... 44	
EXERCISE 6	CAPTURE THE COMMAND "DOWN" 44	
EXERCISE 7	CAPTURE THE COMMAND "DOWN" TEACHING THE DOG TO STOP 45	
EXERCISE 8	TEACHING THE DOG "STAY" 46	
EXERCISE 9	PROMOTE EYE CONTACT 47	
EXERCISE 10	PROMOTING EYE CONTACT WHILE PLAYING 48	
EXERCISE 11	ENCOURAGE EYE CONTACT WITH ANOTHER PERSON 49	
EXERCISE 12	REWARD SPONTANEOUS EYE CONTACT........... 49	
EXERCISE 13	EYE CONTACT BEFORE FOOD RELEASE............. 50	
EXERCISE 14	APPROVED EYE CONTACT (ADVANCED).............51	
EXERCISE 15	IMPULSE CONTROL FOR ADVANCEDLEARNERS .51	
EXERCISE 16	REWARDING CONCENTRATION 52	
EXERCISE 17	10 TREATS GAME..53	
EXERCISE 18	CONCENTRATION PROMOTION AND UTILISATION.. 54	
EXERCISE 19	HIDE AND SEEK GAME 55	

EXERCISE 20   ENCOURAGE THE DOG TO REST 56

EXERCISE 21   IMPULSE CONTROL ON THE BALL 57

EXERCISE 22   BREAK-UP AND STOP COMMAND DURING PLAY 58

EXERCISE 23   STOP COMMAND "NO" - CONDITIONING 58

EXERCISE 24   STRENGTHEN STOP COMMAND – ADVANCED ... 59

EXERCISE 25   BREAK-OFF SIGNAL FOR ADVANCED 60

EXERCISE 26   GENERALISE THE BREAK-OFF SIGNAL 60

EXERCISE 27   BREAKING PLAYTIME 61

6.2 HOUSETRAINING EXERCISES

EXERCISE 28   HOUSETRAINING FOR PUPPIES 62

EXERCISE 29   BOX TRAINING 63

EXERCISE 30   URINATING UPON GREETING 65

EXERCISE 31   NTENSIVE MARKING BEHAVIOUR....................... 66

EXERCISE 32   BLANKET TRAINING 67

6.3 FEEDING BEHAVIOUR

EXERCISE 33   PREVENT FOOD AGGRESSION............................. 68

EXERCISE 34   SWAPS AND "DROP"... 69

EXERCISE 35   FOOD AGGRESSION WITH FEAR 70

EXERCISE 36   PLAYFULLY VARY FEEDING TIMES 71

EXERCISE 37   THE DOG DOES NOT WANT TO EAT 72

EXERCISE 38   BREAKING THE BEGGING HABIT AT THE TABLE .. 72

EXERCISE 39   BREAK THE HABIT OF STEALING FOOD............... 73

EXERCISE 40   BREAKING THE HABIT OF EATING OFF

                   OF THE STREET.. 74

6.4 LEASH HANDLING

EXERCISE 41   GETTING USED TO A HARNESS............................. 75

EXERCISE 42   GOING OUT OF THE HOUSE IN AN ORGANISED FASHION 75

EXERCISE 43   EXERCISE WITH THE DOOR 76

EXERCISE 44   SUCCESS WITHOUT PULLING 77

EXERCISE 45   GETTING RID OF THE TUG 78

EXERCISE 46   SMALL REWARD..78

EXERCISE 47   CHANGE OF DIRECTION 79

EXERCISE 48   A DOG IS TOO DISTRACTED TO MOVE ON 80

EXERCISE 49   OFF-LEASH WALKING - PREPARATION 81

EXERCISE 50   RECALLING THE DOG... 82

EXERCISE 51   CALL THE DOG AT HEEL WITH LURING 83

EXERCISE 52   HEEL WALKING WITH A REWARDING WORD 84

6.5 ENCOUNTER WITH OTHER DOGS

EXERCISE 53   PASSING OTHER DOGS 85

EXERCISE 54   DOG STIFFENS IN FRONT OF OTHER DOGS 86

EXERCISE 55   LEADING THE DOG ON THE AVERTED SIDE 87

EXERCISE 56   THREATENING DOG 87

EXERCISE 57   ASSOCIATING WITH OTHER DOGS
IN A POSITIVE MANNER 88

6.6 MY DOG IS AFRAID OF...

EXERCISE 58   FEAR OF OTHER DOGS... 90

EXERCISE 59   PREPARING TO STAY ALONE...............................91

EXERCISE 60   CREATE A RESTING PLACE.................................. 92

EXERCISE 61   LEAVING THE FLAT 92

EXERCISE 62   PRACTICE STAYING ALONE 93

EXERCISE 63   CONDITIONED RELAXATION AS
SUPPORT WITH MUSIC.. 94

EXERCISE 64   CONDITIONED RELAXATION WITH AROMA OILS 94

EXERCISE 65   UTILISATION BEFORE STAYING ALONE 96

EXERCISE 66   GETTING USED TO THE CAR 966

EXERCISE 67   GETTING USED TO OPENING THE CAR 97

EXERCISE 68   MAKING THE CAR A COMFORTABLE

        PLACE TO REST 98

EXERCISE 69   RELAXING IN THE CAR 98

EXERCISE 70   THE CAR CLOSES 99

EXERCISE 71   START THE ENGINE 99

EXERCISE 72   THE CAR DRIVES OFF 100

EXERCISE 73   CONTROLLED EXIT FROM THE CAR 101

EXERCISE 74   DOG BARKING IN THE CAR 101

EXERCISE 75   TAKING AWAY THE DOG'S FEAR 102

EXERCISE 76   BARKING AT THE SOUND OF THE BELL 103

EXERCISE 77   DOG AND PERSON IN ONE ROOM 104

EXERCISE 78   FEAR OF THE LIFT 105

EXERCISE 79   FEAR OF HOOVER 106

EXERCISE 80   COUNTERACTING FEAR OF NEW YEAR'S EVE

        AND THUNDERSTORMS 107

EXERCISE 81   NEW YEAR'S EVE MEASURES 108

6.7 STOPPING YOUR DOG FROM JUMPING AT SOMEONE

EXERCISE 82   ACTING WITH FORESIGHT 109

EXERCISE 83   GREET PEOPLE WITHOUT YOUR DOG

        JUMPING ON THEM 110

EXERCISE 84   DON'T LET PUPPIES JUMP AT ALL 111

EXERCISE 85   USE TREATS PRECISELY 111

EXERCISE 86   THE SEAT CAN – CONDITIONING 112

EXERCISE 87   THE SEAT CAN TO PREVENT JUMPING PEOPLE .112

EXERCISE 88   PLAYING WITH THE DOG 113

6.8 DOGS' LANGUAGE: BARKING / WHINING
EXERCISE 89   BARK WHEN IT RINGS 2 115
EXERCISE 90   CREATE AN ALTERNATIVE
                    BEHAVIOUR TO BARKING 115
EXERCISE 91   DOGS THAT BARK BECAUSE OF
                    HALLWAY NOISES 116
EXERCISE 92   STOPPING FENCE BARKING WITH THE
                    COMMAND "STOP" 117
EXERCISE 93   DOG BARKING FOR ATTENTION 117
EXERCISE 94   PUPPIES WHINE / HOWL / SQUEAL
                    FOR ATTENTION 118
EXERCISE 95   ADULT DOG WHINE/YELP/SQUEAL
                    FOR ATTENTION 119

6.9 BITING AND SNAPPING
EXERCISE 96   TRAINING PUPPY BITE INHIBITION 120
EXERCISE 97   ADULT DOG SNAPS 121
EXERCISE 98   MUZZLE TRAINING 122

6.10 HUNTING INSTINCT
EXERCISE 99   SEARCH FOR OBJECTS 124
EXERCISE 100   POSITIVE REINFORCEMENT – AVOIDING
                    HUNTING AVOIDANCE OF GAME AND CO 125
EXERCISE 101   LAYING A TRAIL TO REPLACE HUNTING
                    FOR GAME 125
EXERCISE 102   HERDING DOG CHASES CAR/SCOOTER/
                    BICYCLE 126
EXERCISE 103   DOG CHASES SQUIRRELS AND CO. 127

6.11 PRACTICAL CITY TRAINING

EXERCISE 104   LIFT RIDE... 128

EXERCISE 105   WAITING AT THE TRAFFIC LIGHTS 129

EXERCISE 106   WAITING AT THE PLATFORM 129

EXERCISE 107   WAITING FOR THE BUS AND TRAIN 130

EXERCISE 108   RESIST ODOURS 131

EXERCISE 109   RESIST ODOURS VARIATION 131

EXERCISE 110   WALKING UP THE STAIRS....................................132

EXERCISE 111   WALKING DOWN THE STAIRS 132

EXERCISE 112   RELAXING IN THE PARK..133

EXERCISE 113   VISITING A RESTAURANT 134

EXERCISE 114   THE PERFECT OFFICE DOG.................................134

EXERCISE 115   MAILBOX...135

EXERCISE 116   SET-UP OF THE CHIN TARGET 136

6.12 USEFUL EXERCISES: EVERYDAY LIFE, HYGIENE, VET

EXERCISE 117   EXAMINING THE EYES VIA THE CHIN TARGET....137

EXERCISE 118   GETTING THE DOG USED TO EXAMINATIONS ...137

EXERCISE 119   DRY WITH A TOWEL 138

EXERCISE 120   BEING LIFTED ONTO THE TABLE 138

EXERCISE 121   GETTING USED TO THE VET 139

EXERCISE 122   CALM LATERAL POSITION..................................139

EXERCISE 123   BATHING THE DOG... 140

EXERCISE 124   INDOOR SPORTS WITH THE DOG, SQUATS........141

7 BONUS EXERCISES: BRAIN GAMES FOR DOGS

BONUS EXERCISE 1   CLASSIC TREAT THROWING GAME..........143

BONUS EXERCISE 2   TOILET ROLL GAME 1 144

BONUS EXERCISE 3   TOILET ROLL GAME 2 144

BONUS EXERCISE 4   THE CLASSIC SNIFFING RUG 145

BONUS EXERCISE 5   HIDING TREATS INDOORS.......................145

BONUS EXERCISE 6   THE TOWEL WHIRLPOOL 146

BONUS EXERCISE 7   HIDE AND SEEK AT HOME 146

BONUS EXERCISE 8   NEWSPAPER BALLS.................................147

BONUS EXERCISE 9   TREAT SEARCH IN TOYS PARADISE 147

BONUS EXERCISE 10   THE LITTLE HATS GAME............................148

BONUS EXERCISE 11   AMBUSHING AND HUNTING PREY..........148

BONUS EXERCISE 12   THE TREE TRACK 149

BONUS EXERCISE 13   HIDE AND SEEK IN THE FOREST.............149

BONUS EXERCISE 14   THE SNIFFING COURSE 150

BONUS EXERCISE 15   TRICK TRAINING "TURN YOURSELF" 150

BONUS EXERCISE 16   SLALOM THROUGH THE LEGS 151

BONUS EXERCISE 17   PLAY HIDE AND SEEK TOGETHER...........152

BONUS EXERCISE 18   SEARCH GAME WITH GRID BALL.............152

BONUS EXERCISE 19   TREAT DIVING..153

BONUS EXERCISE 20   WHICH HAND? 153

BONUS EXERCISE 21   GIVE YOUR DOG A MASSAGE......................1

DISCLAIMER

This book contains the opinions and ideas of the author and is intended to provide people with helpful and informative knowledge. The strategies may not suit every reader, and there is no guarantee that they will work for everyone. The use of this book and the implementation of the information contained therein are expressly at the reader's own risk. Liability claims against the author for damages of a material or non-material nature caused by the use or non-use of the information or by the use of incorrect and incomplete information are expressly excluded. The work, including all contents, provides no guarantee or warranty for the information's topicality, correctness, completeness and quality. Misprints and misinformation cannot be excluded entirely.

IMPRINT

Unabridged edition 2022 - 1st edition: May 2022

ISBN: 978-3-9824677-6-4

©2022 Miriam Sommer - Information according to §5 TMG The author is represented by: Marklet, Jessica Scollo, Luise-Zietz Str. 116, 12683 Berlin, Germany. Info@siimpo.de, Tax No. 33/529/01238, Ust.Id DE343186079

Stock images: Istockphoto.com
Illustrations: Wasiq-designs
Translation: Sumerna Hassan
Proofreading: Tim Fleischer & Jules Bold
Printing: Amazon Germany or partner

Made in the USA
Monee, IL
30 August 2023

41375943R00111